13

CRIME SCENES BEYOND BOSTON

13 Most Haunted

CRIME SCENES BEYOND BOSTON

Sam Baltrusis

Copyright © 2016 by Sam Baltrusis
All rights reserved

Cover photo by Frank C. Grace, Trig Photography

First published 2016

Manufactured in the United States

ISBN 978-1537467399

Library of Congress CIP data applied for.

All rights reserved. No part of this book may be reproduced or transmitted in any form whatsoever without prior written permission from the publisher except in the case of brief quotations embodied in critical articles and reviews.

CONTENTS

ACKNOWLEDGEMENTS ix
INTRODUCTION xi
RIVERSIDE CEMETERY 1
DOGTOWN 8
OLD SALEM JAIL 16
HARVARD UNIVERSITY 25
CASTLE ISLAND 34
METROPOLITAN STATE HOSPITAL 39
HAWTHORNE COVE MARINA 45
COMMERCIAL STREET 50
FREETOWN STATE FOREST 59
GARDNER-PINGREE HOUSE 66
ORLEANS WATERFRONT INN 72
USS SALEM 78
LIZZIE BORDEN'S HOUSE 86
CONCLUSION 94
SOURCES 101

ACKNOWLEDGEMENTS

After writing *13 Most Haunted Crime Scenes Beyond Boston*, I can say without hesitation that this book is my most terrifying so far. Special thanks to Joni Mayhan, author of *Bones in the Basement*, for penning the first chapter. Her wisdom and hands-on experience at several of the state's most-haunted locations is featured throughout the manuscript. Also, I would like to thank Peter Muise, author of *Legends and Lore of the North Shore*, for writing the second chapter on New England's other witch city, Dogtown. Photographers Frank C. Grace and Jason Baker deserve a supernatural slap on the back for capturing the eerie aesthetic of the main haunts in the *13 Most Haunted* countdown. Ed Maas, the owner of the family-runned Orleans Waterfront Inn, also deserves major props for opening his extremely haunted doors to my research team, which included Mike Cultrera, my partner in crime. Major thanks to the handful of paranormal investigators and researchers who helped make *13 Most Haunted Crime Scenes* a reality, including Laura Giuliano and Michael Baker from Para-Boston, my friends and well-respected investigators Rachel Hoffman, Tina Storer and Kassie Kreitman from Paranormal Xpeditions, Ron Kolek and Anne Kerrigan from *Ghost Chronicles* and Adam Berry from Destination America's *Kindred Spirits*. My high-school journalism teacher, Beverly Reinschmidt, also deserves kudos for inspiring me to keep writing. Thanks to my mother, Deborah Hughes Dutcher, for being there when I need her most and my friends for their continued support. The team at MATV's Neighborhood View, including Anne D'Urso-Rose, Ron Cox and my *What's New?* co-host Sharon Fillyaw, deserve an old-school high five for helping me with the TV show component of the project. Salem is a major player in this paranormal-themed travel guide, so I would like to thank the team from Essex Heritage for encouraging me to return to the "Witch City," including Ryan McMahon, Kathryn Rutkowski and Robyn Giannopolo.

INTRODUCTION

When I first jumped off of the vessel *Naumkeag* on the rocky coastline of the once off-limits Bakers Island, I started to hyperventilate. I could see in my mind's eye a young girl, probably around 13-years-old. She was wearing late nineteenth century garb and, from what I picked up that particularly windy June morning in Salem Harbor, she was waiting for me.

While doing research for *13 Most Haunted Crime Scenes Beyond Boston*, I signed up to lead weekend tours to the allegedly haunted island. After a nightmarish season in the so-called "Witch City" during the Halloween season of 2013 before writing my book *Ghosts of Salem*, I swore I would never go back to the North Shore haunt that turned inexplicably dark, and oddly evil, as the season progressed.

Bakers Island remained in the hands of the Colonial government until 1660, when the General Court granted a request by the town of Salem to annex both Bakers and Misery islands. *Photo by Frank C. Grace.*

I'm back. Well, kinda sorta. The sixty-acre island is about five miles off the coast of Salem. While I did do some preliminary research on Bakers Island, I had no clue about its haunted past. As we inched toward the rocks, I intuitively knew that I was about to step on a paranormally active hot spot. The ghost girl was waiting ... and so was a living man.

The lightkeeper, Bill, greeted our vessel as we quietly landed ashore. Wearing what looked like a Harley Davidson T-shirt, Bill was standing on the rocks, holding a garbage bag while Essex National Heritage's chief executive officer, Annie, quickly hopped off onto the slippery shore. "No ghost stories," Annie told me a few minutes before landing. The salty waters of the harbor spit in my face as *Naumkeag*'s captain John maneuvered past Marblehead during my first trip to Salem's shutter island. I had asked Annie if she knew the story of the Screeching Woman of Lovis Cove. "Never heard of it," she said with a familiar New England nod that oddly reminded me of Katharine Hepburn. I sheepishly smiled back.

When I spotted the ghost girl on Bakers Island, I decided to keep it a secret. As far as I knew, there were no deaths at the lighthouse that had been closed to the general public for seventy years. Besides, I promised my boss no ghost stories. I couldn't help myself.

Lightkeeper Bill did write about what he later referred to as a "gremlin" on Bakers.

"When I got to the beach I was going to row out to the *Whaler* and take a look at the engine," he wrote online a few days before my first visit. "The oars were gone. Brenda and I remember placing them in the boat and I then jammed them in to make sure they stayed. Two life jackets and a pair of shoes were untouched but the oars were gone. I can only assume that someone stole them. Pretty lousy."

Stolen oars? It's possible. However, my intuition suggested something else, a poltergeist. Whatever it was, the spirit wanted to play.

The *Naumkeag* came carrying gifts, several pieces of wood needed to build a makeshift gift shop on the island. As I explored the island's lighthouse, I had one of my *That's So Raven* moments. I somehow psychically replayed what seemed to be a horrific maritime tragedy. However, the ghost girl on the island was letting me know that she was fine and that she has found postmortem serenity there even though she died tragically more than one century ago.

According to local legend, Bakers Island was named after a man who was mysteriously killed on the island by a falling tree. While there's no proof of the story told by the late historian Edward Rowe Snow, we do know of a man named Robert Baker who was fatally hit by a piece of lumber in 1640 in the shipyard off of Salem. The island was deeded to Salem in 1660 and rented out to John Turner in 1670. For the record, Turner was famous for building the House of the Seven Gables. On April 8, 1796, President George Washington agreed to appropriate $6,000 for a lighthouse and a beacon was first lit on January 3, 1798. In 1820, the original light was replaced with a pair of lighthouses known as "Ma and Pa" or "Mr. and Mrs." Unfortunately, the shorter "Ma" tower was demolished in 1922.

In the late nineteenth century, Bakers Island became home to a fifty-room hotel called Winne-Eagan, which opened in 1888 and burned completely to the ground from an accidental fire in 1906.

Bakers Island Light Station is located on Bakers Island in Salem Sound, a 60-acre island with a large summer colony. *Photo by Frank C. Grace.*

As far as ghost lore, Bakers Island is legendary. For years, the fog horn would sound off without provocation and flickering lights were seen on the island when it was vacant during the off-season. There were also sightings of a horse spirit near the lighthouse. Visitors have reported the smell of hay and disembodied sounds usually associated with four-legged equines like whinnying and hoof stomping.

"Most of the paranormal activity on Bakers Island takes place during the winter months when the island is deserted," wrote Lee Holloway in *Ghosts of the Massachusetts Lights*. "Caretakers have heard what sounds like a party emanating from the Chase Cottage. Workers in the Wells Cottage have been attacked by a 'kissing ghost' and lights are sometimes seen in the general store and Nicholson house when both are closed for the season."

The ghost of Naomi Coyler, who died during a swim off of Bakers Island during the 1960s, is said to haunt the island. There's also a story of a jewel thief who supposedly hid his booty on Bakers. The mysterious flickering orbs are said to be the privateer looking for his buried treasure. In the late 1990s, a group of paranormal investigators reached out to the tightly-guarded summer home community to investigate the so-called evil entity known as the "beast of Bakers Island." However, the paranormal team quickly packed up their belongings and fled once they found out the island doesn't have electricity.

So, what about my encounter with the ghost girl? On the Fourth of July in 1898, a two-level vessel picked up a large group of visitors from Bakers Island and, after dropping off passengers at Salem Willows, tragically capsized en route to Beverly. "The small excursion steamer *Surf City*, with about 60 passengers on board ... was struck by a sudden, but terrible, squall last evening and capsized," reported the *Fitchburgh Sentinel* on July 5, 1898. "The scene, while the work of rescue was going on, was a fearful one, as over half of those on board were women, and their screams could be heard for miles. Many clung to the top of the hurricane deck and supported themselves until the boats came, while others grasped the flag staffs and even the smoke stack."

The majority of the passengers survived the disaster, but eight women and children died, including two teen girls and several unnamed children.

My theory is that the ghost girl on Bakers Island is somehow related to the *Surf City* tragedy of 1898.

My stint giving tours on Bakers Island was short lived. After months of interviews and approvals from the Coast Guard, I only lasted one weekend. I told my boss that the ten-hour workday was too much for me to handle. Truthfully, I was legitimately freaked out by the ghosts still lingering on Bakers Island.

I was moved to the mainland and returned to the city that haunted my dreams for years. Essex Heritage asked me to give their "Myths & Misconceptions" tour in downtown Salem during the summer of 2016. My fingers were crossed that the ghosts from my past would leave me alone.

Known for its annual Halloween "Haunted Happenings" gathering, it's no surprise that the historic Massachusetts seaport is considered to be one of New England's most haunted destinations. With city officials emphasizing its not-so-dark past, tourists from all over the world seem to focus on the wicked intrigue surrounding the 1692 witch trials.

As far as the paranormal is concerned, the city is considered to be hallowed ground.

Originally called Naumkeag, Salem means "peace." However, as its historical legacy dictates, the city was anything but peaceful during the late seventeenth century. In fact, when accused witch and landowner Giles Corey was pressed to death over a two-day period, he allegedly cursed the sheriff and the city. Over the years, his specter has allegedly been spotted preceding disasters in Salem, including the fire that destroyed most of the downtown area in June 1914. Based on my research, a majority of the hauntings conjured up in Salem over the city's tumultuous three-hundred-year-old history have ties to disaster, specifically the one-hundred-year-old fire that virtually annihilated the once prosperous North Shore seaport.

Cursed? Salem is full of secrets.

My first ghost tour experience in Salem was an impromptu trek on Mollie Stewart's "Spellbound" tour in 2010. I remember gazing up at the allegedly haunted Joshua Ward House and being convinced I had seen a spirit looking out of the second-floor window. It turned out to be a bust of George Washington. Soon after writing my first book, *Ghosts of*

Boston, I signed on to give historical-based ghost tours of my own in a city that both excited and scared me. I let Salem's spirits guide me.

One of my first face-to-face encounters with a negative entity was at the Joshua Ward House. I felt a warm sensation on my chest one night in September 2012 while I was giving a ghost tour. It felt like a spider bite. However, I wasn't prepared for the bitter truth. After the tour, I lifted up my shirt and noticed three cat-like scratch marks on my chest. In the paranormal world, this is called the "mark of intrinity" and it's said to signify the touch of a demonic entity. I was terrified.

The Joshua Ward House at 148 Washington St. in Salem was purchased by Lark Hotels and was transformed into a boutique hotel called "The Merchant" in 2015. *Photo by Frank C. Grace.*

After the incident, I refused to get too close to the haunted and potentially evil structure.

In 2015, the Joshua Ward House at 148 Washington St. was purchased by Lark Hotels and was transformed into a boutique hotel. Renamed "The Merchant," the posh overnight haunt celebrates Salem's rich maritime past. No mention of the reported ghosts and demonic entity allegedly lurking in the shadows of this chic new hot spot.

Are the new owners in complete denial of the structure's haunted history? Probably.

Listed on the National Register of Historical Places in 1978, the three-floor Federal-style building had a stint as the Washington Hotel in the late nineteenth century. It stood vacant for years and was restored in the late '70s. When Carlson Realty moved into the historic house, mysterious events started to occur. Chairs, lampshades, trashcans and candlesticks would be found turned upside down when the staff arrived in the morning. Papers were strewn on the floor, and candles were bent in the shape of an "S." One of the offices on the second floor is ice cold, a telltale sign of paranormal activity.

Why would the Joshua Ward House be haunted?

The structure was built on the foundation of Sheriff George Corwin's old house, and many people believe the venerated sheriff's spirit lingers at the 148 Washington St. locale. In fact, his body was buried beneath the building but was later interred at Broad Street Cemetery.

After mysteriously dying from a heart attack at age thirty, the younger Corwin was arguably the city's most despised man and rightfully so. The then 20-something sheriff reportedly got a kick out of torturing the men and women accused of witchcraft. Although it was the uncle, Magistrate Jonathan Corwin, who tried and accused the innocents, it was the sick and twisted nephew who enforced the unjust verdicts.

"Sheriff Corwin was so disliked by the people of Salem, that when he died of a heart attack in 1696, his family didn't dare bury him in the cemetery for fear he'd be dug up and his body torn limb from limb," wrote Robert Ellis Cahill, himself a former Essex County sheriff turned author, in *Haunted Happenings.* Corwin's cruelty is legendary. For example, he sent an officer to accused witch Mary Parker's home in Andover on September 23, 1692, literally the day after her execution, demanding that her son fork over the dead woman's farm and goods. Parker's son, who was still mourning the loss of his mother, had to cough up a large sum of money to stop Corwin's demands for corn, hay and cattle.

Luckily, the "Myths & Misconceptions" tour I lead on the weekends focused more on history and less on Salem's ghosts. Oddly, many of the haunts from my past—including Essex Heritage's main office at 10

Federal Street—ended up on the tour. Yes, Essex Heritage's office had a past life as Salem's Old Witch Gaol.

During the witch trials hysteria, the John Ward House was literally across the street from the dungeon and is reportedly haunted by tortured spirits from Salem's 1692 past. *Photo by Frank C. Grace.*

The original dungeon in which the accused witches were held was constructed between 1683 and 1684. The subterranean jail was 70 by 280 feet and was made of hand-hewn, oak timbers and siding. The conditions in the prison were notoriously horrific. Prisoners were held in small cells with no bedding. There were no bars on the cells, but if the prisoners ran away from their punishment, they were generally caught and immediately executed.

Prisoners were charged for straw bedding and food, and if they could not afford them, they did without. Water was also withheld from prisoners since the Puritans believed they would be able to get more "confessions" if the prisoners were thirsty. The salaries of the sheriff, magistrate and hangman were also paid by the prisoners, and they were billed for cuffs and other bonds and even for the torturous acts of searching their bodies of witchery "marks" and getting their heads shaved in the process.

At least five died from the inhumane conditions in the dungeon. It's also notoriously haunted.

There's supposedly a prison guard–type apparition making his nightly rounds. His image has been caught on camera. Adam Page, investigator with F.I.N.D. Paranormal, said he has proof there's an angry sentinel spirit guarding the former Witch Gaol site. "The old guard at 10 Federal Street is really angry," said Page, a former case manager with Paranormal Salem. "We always run into his full-bodied apparition at that building."

Page said during his days working at Paranormal Salem, he would get a bad vibe from the Colonial-era sentinel. "The full-bodied apparition we caught at 10 Federal was walking straight down the hallway," Page explained. "He didn't see us, so I think he's more of a residual haunting. But he could be intelligent. If you look in the door, he walked right to left."

I was happy to learn that the "Myths & Misconceptions" tour was based in the Salem Visitor Center on New Liberty Street and not the Old Witch Gaol location. And, yes, the old Salem Armory building is also allegedly haunted. However, it's more of a residual energy relating to a five-alarm fire that destroyed most of the structure on February 22, 1982.

On one of my recent "Myths & Misconceptions" tours, a woman from California flipped out when I spoke in front of Salem's Town Hall. Home to the reenactment of Bridget Bishop's trial called *Cry Innocent*, the historic structure is famous for the dance sequence in the movie Hocus Pocus. It's also where I launched my third book, *Ghosts of Salem: Haunts of the Witch City*. The out-of-town visitor on my tour swore she saw two ghostly faces pressed against the window on the second floor of Town Hall as if they were intently listening to what I said. I nodded when she told me. "Yep, I know the ghosts of Salem are listening," I said followed by a nervous laugh. She had no clue what I've seen.

While Salem is a hotbed for paranormal activity, it wasn't always an open-and-shut case when it came to my search for the most haunted crime scenes in Eastern Massachusetts. Not every murder scene is haunted. And not every victim turned psychic imprint is based on actual fact. In some cases, a horrific backstory was completely fabricated or twisted over time to explain the supernatural.

With a few haunts featured in *13 Most Haunted Crimes Scenes Beyond Boston*, I had to dig deep for the skeletal secrets buried deep beneath the Bay State's blood-stained soil. Based purely on its unsubstantiated lore, some locations didn't make the cut. However, it doesn't always mean there isn't some truth behind the legends.

Joni Mayhan, author of *Bones in the Basement*, believes that crime scenes have the potential for a residual haunting based purely on its bloody backstory. "I believe that locations of tragic events are more prone to a haunting than any other location." she told me. "When a person dies unexpectedly, sometimes their soul doesn't pass through the white light as it should. The emotions surrounding the event often makes them balk. Sometimes when it happens suddenly, they don't even realize they've died. Other times, they remain because of a sense of guilt or a need to let others know what happened to them."

Mayhan researched the history of the S.K. Pierce Victorian Mansion in Gardner while writing *Bones in the Basement*. According to multiple psychics who visited the location, a female escort was killed in the house. "Supposedly, a prostitute was murdered in the red room of the Haunted Victorian Mansion. Psychic mediums have picked up on her energy over and over again, giving the legend a sense of validity. However, no records show a woman who wasn't a member of the Pierce family dying in the mansion," Mayhan explained.

"Could it have been covered up? Certainly. Wealth and power would provide them with far more means than if it happened to someone of lesser fortune. Some people feel that it happened later in the mansion's timeline, during the time when it was a boarding house or perhaps when it was vacant. If this was the case, she wasn't a resident of the mansion and her body was carried away before anyone could discover the murder," Mayhan continued.

Some crime scenes, she said, aren't haunted because the victims crossed over to the light. "I recently brought my Paranormal 101 class to the murder site of seventeen year-old Patricia Joyce. She disappeared in 1965 while taking a shortcut through the woods around Crystal Lake in Gardner," Mayhan said. "Her body was found thirty feet from the pumping station. It was the first murder in Gardner in fifty-one years and remains unsolved to this day."

Mayhan's class attempted to reach out to the spirit to help solve the cold case. No luck. "Several of my students are talented psychic mediums and none of us were able to connect with Patty's soul. We believe she crossed over immediately, which is sometimes the case. Judging by the information we found in a blog that was written by her sister, Patty was a good girl who typically followed the rules in life. She probably wouldn't have resisted the white light and would have crossed over at the time of her death, like she was supposed to do. The imprint of her death was strong in the area, but we felt it was a residual energy that was absorbed by the location."

Author Nathaniel Hawthorne met his wife, Sophia Peabody Hawthorne, at a lavish dinner party at the Grimshawe House, 53 Charter Street, next to the Old Buring Point. *Photo by Frank C. Grace.*

However, not every paranormal expert believes extreme violence psychically imprints itself into the environment.

Michael Baker, a scientific investigator with the group Para-Boston, said there isn't any rhyme or reason why a crime scene would be more paranormally active when compared to other Massachusetts-based haunts. "When we are speaking of interactions with activity alleged to be connected to the existing consciousness of human beings, I would think a more active history would always play a bigger role," Baker explained. "However, in my findings I have not yet seen a correlation between the type of historic activity and proposed hauntings. Much of the connections of violent pasts to haunted locations seems to be more folklore than fact. I'm still not sure what elements of our daily lives leave the biggest impacts."

In other words, Baker believes that a place like Lizzie Borden's later-in-life home Maplecroft has as much potential to be paranormally active as the actual house on Second Street in Fall River where the murders occurred. "The claims of hauntings by the majority seems to be void of elements that directly tie to major historical events," he said, using his data-focused NECAPS report as proof. "We never see Lincoln giving the Gettysburg address for example, and while the battlefields in Gettysburg do seem to produce alleged remnants of battles, that trait does not seem to continue in many other violent locations where paranormal activity is simply footsteps or doors closing," Baker explained.

But some cities in Massachusetts, like Salem with its cursed witch trials past, are more prone to hauntings than others, right? Not exactly.

"People want to find patterns if something doesn't make sense," explained Margaret Press, a Salem-based crime writer and author of *Counterpoint: A Murder in Massachusetts Bay*. "Salem makes it easy for us to find these patterns because of historic accident. It's not in the ground. It's not in the air. It's in ourselves."

Press, who penned the essay "Salem as Crime Scene" in the book *Salem: Place, Myth and Memory*, talked about how thousands of visitors make a pilgrimage to the city every October looking for "the occult, the weird and the unexplained," and they find it. "Despite its name, from the Hebrew word for peace, the tourists who flock to the city are convinced the city is about witches and death," Press wrote. "They buy mugs and T-shirts and wander the museums. But beneath it all they're looking and listening. Salem battled him once. But is Satan really gone for good?"

In Press's world, Salem's emphasis on its "specters and spectacles" has a downside. "We're not training our young people in critical thinking," she said, slamming the city's proliferation of so-called psychics and palm readers. "If people accept pseudo-science or crap science, there's a real practical downside. It's no better than 1692."

However, Press did coin the phrase known as the "Salem factor," which she used to explain the city's abundance of bizarre synchronicities—like how the Great Fire of 1914 oddly started in the exact spot where nineteen innocents were hanged for witchcraft. However, the author believes there are rational explanations for the inexplicable. "We find coincidences and connections in the human experience here because we expect them," she wrote. "We look for the extraordinary in events here and we see it."

Press cites the controversy surrounding Fatima's, a two-decade-old psychic studio in Salem, which made national headlines in 2013 after an employee charged a New York man $16,800 to protect him from a curse, as proof of society's gullibility to Salem's "boo! business." For the record, the man was reimbursed based on a city ordinance stating that psychics can only forecast the future and read the past. Curses are apparently off-limits.

Christian Day, owner of two witch-themed shops in Salem who recently moved back home to New Orleans, didn't like how a local police detective categorized Fatima's Romani style of fortunetelling as fraudulent. "If they're a fraud, then we're all frauds, and all religion is a fraud," Day told the *Boston Globe* on October 31, 2013. "They're not regulating the priest who absolves you of your sins and tells you to put some money in the collection basket, or the old lady who sends all of her money to Pat Robertson. They pick on us for one reason: They're afraid of us. They've always been afraid of us."

Oddly, Press herself made similar headlines when she included a section in her book *Counterpoint* suggesting that legendary Salem witch Laurie Cabot divined the whereabouts of murder victim Martha Brailsford in 1991. The local legend supposedly gave a tip to police about the local woman's accused perpetrator, Tom Maimoni, and then continued to put a binding spell on him. "Laurie closed her eyes and pictured Tom Maimoni in a white cocoon, bound up in a thread of light," Press wrote. When asked about the section in her book about Cabot,

Press shrugged it off. "The press picked up on it and made it sound like Laurie Cabot cracked the case," Press responded. "She didn't."

The Samuel Pickman House, located on the corner of Charter and Liberty Streets, is said to be home to an evil entity connected to a horrific murder committed centuries ago. *Photo by Frank C. Grace.*

Nestled next to the highly trafficked Charter Street Cemetery in Salem, the Samuel Pickman House is now owned by the Peabody Essex Museum. Tour groups, including my weekly "Myths & Misconceptions" tour pass this historic building, and passersby peek through its windows. Several people believe they've seen a full-bodied apparition of a girl peering from the upper-floor window. Others claim the small Colonial-era structure is home to a demonic entity that manifests in photos taken through the seventeenth-century building's old-school windows.

One ghastly story tells of a husband and wife who lived in the Samuel Pickman House with their seven-year-old daughter. Similar to the demonic infestation in Stephen King's *The Shining*, an evil entity is rumored to have caused the husband to go insane.

According to legend, the man chained his daughter up in the attic, torturing and starving the child. He then tied his wife to a tree outside
Mary Corey, the second wife of witch trials victim Giles Corey, is buried in Salem's Old Burying Point. *Photo by Frank C. Grace.*

and killed her by pouring hot wax over her body, leaving her to die a slow, painful death. The possessed man then fled, leaving the dead child in the attic and his murdered-by-wax wife tied to the tree.

People on my walking tours who have taken photos of the house claim it is still inhabited by a demonic force. There are many reports of the ghost of the young girl looking out the attic window at the crowds below.

After doing exhaustive historical research, I found no real proof to suggest that the story of the murder or the supposed demonic infestation at the house is true. However, the building is a surefire hot spot of photographic anomalies, ranging from orbs to a mist that envelops the structure.

Next to the Samuel Pickman House is the Witch Trials Memorial and the old cemetery. My most profound encounter in Salem several years ago was at the Old Burying Point on Charter Street. I spotted a full-bodied apparition of a lady in white coming from what I learned later was the gravestone of Giles Corey's second wife, Mary. It's my theory that Mary Corey's residual energy is looking for her husband. She's heading oddly toward the very spot located at the present-day Howard Street Cemetery where the stubborn but determined old man was crushed to death. Yes, love does exist in the afterlife.

While historians have agreed that Corey was pressed to death near the Old Salem Jail, they've been unsure about the execution site where nineteen innocent men and women were hanged for witchcraft in 1692.

Apparently, "x" does mark the spot and it's located behind a Walgreen's.

Salem earned international ink, once again, in early 2016 after a crew of experts supposedly pinpointed the exact location of the gallows. For the record, I wrote about the "Proctor's Ledge" location in 2013. "One piece of new evidence emerged from court notes dating back to August 1692," I wrote in *Ghosts of Salem*. "Rebecca Eames, a woman suspected of witchcraft who was taken from her home in Boxford, said she saw the gallows from Boston Street while on her way to downtown Salem. The latest theory is that the true site is located behind the Walgreen's located at 59 Boston Street."

It was this historical document from Eames that was used to identify the location of Gallows Hill.

As far as how they were executed, historians aren't sure if the hangings were on locust trees, which were probably not strong enough for an execution, or if the accused were hanged from traditional gallows. "Contemporary accounts make clear that the prisoners uttered their last words, with nooses around their necks, from ladders," wrote Frances Hill in *Hunting for Witches*. "When the ladder was pushed away from whatever it was leaning on, they died a slow, painful death. But whether the ladder was supported by a branch or a scaffold, the sources do not say."

Bridget Bishop was the first person executed for witchcraft during the Salem witch trials of 1692. During the hysteria, 72 people were accused and 20 people were executed. *Photo by Frank C. Grace.*

There is also debate about the skeletal remains of the victims. "Bone fragments have been found," said a representative from the Peabody Essex Museum about an excavation at Gallows Hill Park, "but we'll never really know what they were from." At least three victims from 1692—Rebecca Nurse, John Proctor and George Jacobs—were brought back by relatives, salvaged in the wee hours of the night and given a proper burial. The remains of the other seventeen victims, which have been the subject of rumors that they were exhumed and relocated by wealthy merchant Phillip English and other theories claiming they were buried beneath the cellar of a church in nearby Marblehead, are believed to be dumped in either a ditch or within the rocky crevices of Proctor's Ledge.

Kathryn Rutkowski, visitor services manager with Essex Heritage and creator of the "Myths & Misconceptions" tour, brought me to the granite bench honoring the first victim executed in Salem during the 1692 witch trials hysteria. Her name? Bridget Bishop.

Bishop lived in Salem Village (present-day Danvers) but owned property on the eastern side of Salem's current Washington and Church Streets. As far as witchcraft, several men accused her of dabbling in the dark arts. John Cook Jr., an eighteen-year-old who lived on Essex Street, just opposite First Church, claimed he was awakened one morning by Bishop's specter, which was grinning at him. She "struck me on the side of the head, which did hurt me very much," he claimed. Bishop allegedly returned and caused an apple to fly from Cook's hand into his mother's lap.

Cook's neighbor, Samuel Shattuck, testified that Bishop's lacy garb was un-Christian, and when she visited the Stattuck home, their son began crying and became "stupefied and devoid of reason." Born Bridget Playfer, Bishop married Samuel Wasselbee and had two children. Her entire family, husband and children, died under mysterious circumstances. In 1664, Bishop married Thomas Oliver and had a daughter, Christian. Oliver also died, and Bishop remarried to Edward Bishop, hence her namesake.

Yes, the woman had a checkered past.

She was known as a penny pincher, and a local Salem woman claimed in 1682 that Bishop's specter, with Alice Parker, who was also accused and executed as a witch, pulled her down to the beach and tried to drown her. Of course, this was ten years before the trials and a precursor to the accusations that would ultimately lead to her demise on June 10, 1692.

Historically, Bishop is credited with running a scandalous tavern near the present-day Lyceum. However, it's more likely that she's been confused over time with Sarah and Edward Bishop, who ran a watering hole out of their home down the street. They were sent to Boston's less-strict jail and managed to escape.

Bridget Bishop wasn't so lucky.

At her trial on March 24, 1692, several witnesses testified that a poltergeist attack took place as Bishop was being taken past the town meetinghouse, a stone's throw from her Salem home and the present-day location of Turner's Seafood at Lyceum Hall. "A demon invisibly entered the meeting house, tore down part of it, so there was no person to be seen, yet the people, at the noise, running in, found a board which was strongly fastened with several nails, transported into another quarter of the house," wrote one eyewitness. In other words, spirits were supposedly active during the thirteen months of mass hysteria and were so powerful that a wooden board levitated across the room.

My first paranormal experience in Salem involved Bishop. Soon after I wrote Ghosts of Boston, I signed on to give historical-based ghost tours of my own in a city that both excited and terrified me. I let Salem's spirits guide me. I had several odd experiences outside of Lyceum Hall, which was said to be Bridget Bishop's tavern.

However, it was her orchard. An apple mysteriously rolled out of nowhere in the alley behind what is now Turner's Seafood. I looked up. No one was there. I accepted it as a peace offering from Bishop.

My perceptions of Bishop has changed since my first encounter with what I believed to be her ghost in 2013.

Rutkowski and I talked about the misconceptions associated with the only victim hanged alone. "Out of all of the executions, we know the most about Bridget," Rutkowski told me in early June which was oddly the day before the anniversary of Bishop's murder. Rutkowski and I started tearing up when we talked about the crimes against humanity that unfolded in Salem in 1692. "They could have just put the noose around Bridget's neck and killed her instantly," she emoted. "But they didn't. The executioners actually positioned the noose so she would die a slow, horrible death. She was hanging in the gallows—convulsing and losing control of her bowels—in front of a crowd of people. They were publicly shaming her before they killed her."

As we talked, I fought to hold back the tears. I was shivering in the beauty and the madness of the moment. I had the ultimate realization.

The most haunted crime scene in Massachusetts? I was standing in the middle of New England's deepest, darkest secret. It's Salem.

The bronze statue of Roger Conant, founder of Salem, was unveiled in 1913.
Photo by Sam Baltrus

Chapter 1

RIVERSIDE CEMETERY
BARRE
MOST HAUNTED: #13

"Heaven won't take me."
—EVP captured by Joni Mayhan, author and paranormal investigator

As we stepped into the cemetery, it was apparent that something bad once happened there. The energy hung in the air like a bank of fog, surging around us as if trying to get our attention. I allowed the energy to connect and immediately saw a young woman who feared for her life. I knew in an instant that she lost her life in this forest.

The land has a way of holding onto energy. Some of it is good. When you go there, you feel instantly comfortable. Other places hold onto other emotions. As a paranormal investigator, I recognize much of it as residual energy. It isn't necessarily haunted in the sense that most people identify with. It's just there, resounding like an imprint on the land.

For someone with metaphysical gifts, it's apparent. We feel the energy and find ourselves identifying it before we even notice the scenery. One such place is the former town of Coldbrook Village.

Coldbrook Springs was once a bustling town with two hotels, a bowling alley, a blacksmith shop, post office, billiard hall, a box mill, school, and nearly 35 houses. It was removed in the 1930s as part of the Quabbin Reservoir project. The state bought all of the buildings and demolished them to provide a clean watershed for the Ware River, which flows into the Quabbin Reservoir and provides drinking water to Boston and its suburbs. People were relocated to nearby towns of Oakham, Barre and Hubbardston, and the town simply ceased to exist.

Besides a few foundations, the cemetery is virtually all that remains of the old town. We walked the grounds, taking in the mixture of old and new headstones. Birds chirped in the distance as the wind rustled through the tops of the tall pines. At the back of the cemetery we found a monument to the Naramore children, who were killed by their own mother in 1901. We spend a quiet moment reading the inscription.

Poverty stricken and living with an abusive husband, Elizabeth Naramore went to the town for help. When officials visited the residence, they determined that the children would need to be put into foster homes. Before they could do that, Elizabeth killed them, from oldest to youngest, and then attempted unsuccessfully to commit suicide. A monument was erected in the 1990s to remember the lost children. It's hard to stand there and not feel a rush of emotion. Over time, the stone has gained a collection of toys and small cars, left by saddened visitors.

As we walked back towards the entrance, I was drawn to a group of three tombstones.

They were old and faded, the words difficult to make out on the worn slate stone. The first stone listed the name of a Catherine Sibley, who lived from 1805 to 1874. Beside her grave was the grave of her husband, Captain Charles Sibley, who lived from 1808 to 1849. And sadly, beside his was the grave of their four children. This was what caused me to pause.

They were listed, one after another, telling a heartbreaking story.

- James died on October 9, 1843 at nine months old.
- Catherine died on September 19, 1847 at six years, five months.
- Mary died the day after her sister, on September 20, 1847 at the age of two years, seven months.
- Charles died the day after Christmas on the same year, December 26, 1847 at the age of twelve years, seven months.

We just stood there, taking it all in, trying to wrap our minds around the tragedy of losing four children, two of whom died within a day of one

Entrance to Riverside Cemetery in Barre. *Photo by Jason Baker.*

another. How did they die? Was there a horrible disease that swept through the area, taking their children one by one, teasing them to believe that one would survive, only to have him taken from them the day after Christmas? My heart went out to their parents.

The Naramore grave in Riverside Cemetery in Barre is usually surrounded by toys and offerings to the victims of the filicide. *Photo by Jason Baker.*

I'm always very respectful of the dead, and with this comes a sense of compassion. As a paranormal investigator, I know that not all of the souls pass on like they're supposed to. When faced with a tragic death, some lose their way and become earthbound. We wanted to make sure this wasn't the case. We pulled out our digital recorders and conducted a short EVP session.

"Captain Sibley, are you still here?" Sandy asked.

The response was heart wrenching. "Yes. Heaven won't take me."

The EVP is faint and must be listened to with headphones on high volume. For reasons I can't explain, the audio has faded over the years, perhaps from being transferred too many times, or possibly for other reasons. Maybe I was the only one meant to hear it.

After listening to it, I couldn't stop thinking about this poor family and the possibility that the father was still lingering around his grave over one-hundred and sixty years later. I went back to his grave the following week.

In the quiet of the cemetery, I sat beside his headstone and just talked to him. I didn't know if he was listening or not, but I wanted to help him if I could. I told him about the natural process of what happens to us after death.

"When we die, we're supposed to cross over into the white light, moving to the place where we're supposed to go. Some people call it Heaven," I said. I looked around at the quiet bank of trees, wondering if he was there, or if I was simply talking to myself. I had to continue though.

My voice sounded like a prayer as I began speaking again. "Look for the white light. It's right above you. All your family is waiting for you. Call out to them to help you cross through." I took a deep breath and then added something I hoped would help. "God loves you and welcomes you with open arms. Go find the peace and serenity you deserve." And then I cried.

I went back several weeks later to see if he was still there. I turned on my digital voice recorder and asked again. "Captain Sibley, are you still here?" Later when I listened to the recording, all I heard was the sound of birds chirping in the background. If he was still there, he wasn't responding. I hoped he'd listened to my advice and found the peace he so deserved. For insurance, a year later I brought a psychic medium to the cemetery and he crossed over five souls. My hope was that if Captain Sibley hadn't crossed over initially, that he'd gone when the psychic medium gave him another opportunity. Either way, I truly feel he finally found his way.

The story would have ended there if I'd been able to let it go. Thoughts of the Sibley family haunted me. I couldn't get them off my mind. I reached out to a friend who has a knack for researching and she was able to provide me with more information. She filled in many of the details for me, fleshing out the bare-boned tragedy and giving it life.

The Sibleys had a long history in Massachusetts. They arrived in Salem in 1629, quickly becoming a very prominent family. They boasted statesmen and soldiers of the Revolutionary War, as well as being prosperous business owners. An early relative of Charles Sibley's was Mary Woodrow Sibley, who allegedly showed Tituba and Indian John how to make the urine cakes used to test for witches during the Salem Witch Trials.

Nearly two centuries later, Charles Sibley was born in 1808, the youngest of five siblings. The family relocated to Barre, Massachusetts while he was a child, setting up a homestead just outside of Coldbrook Springs. When he was 25 years-old, he married a woman named Catharine Brigham who was three years his senior. He was listed as "Captain Sibley" on his gravestone, but no information could be found about any military services. In colonial times, this was often added to the name because of the family's past military service.

The unspeakable story of the Naramore family and the events of March 21, 1901 has been laid to rest with the bodies of the six children who were buried in the paupers' corner of Riverside Cemetery on Granger Road. *Photo by Jason Baker.*

They were married for two years before having their first child, a son they named Charles, after his father. Three years later, they would have another son named Nelson. Daughter, Catherine, was born two afterward, named after her mother. The following year, they would add another son, James, to the family, but he would die of whooping cough before his first birthday. In 1845, they would have a second daughter they named Mary. And in 1848 they would have their last child, who they would also name Charles.

They would lose all but two of their children soon after to dysentery.

Dying of dysentery was a very horrible way to go. An inflammation of the lower intestines would lead to a high fever and painful, never-ending diarrhea. Left untreated, the victim would become dehydrated and eventually succumb to the infection. It is often caused by consuming contaminated food or water, or from poor hygiene. Charles himself would die two years later from Typhoid Fever, after being sick for eight straight days.

Charles' wife, Catherine would live to be sixty-nine, dying in 1874 in Boston. Her death certificate listed paralysis as the cause of death, although I'm sure there's more to the story. Sons, Nelson and Charles (the second) would survive both of their parents. Nelson married in 1870 and died in 1900. Charles married in 1882 and died sometime after 1930 in Highgate, Vermont. His occupation was listed as a paper carrier.

There is still so much I don't know about the Sibley family, and I'm certain this won't be the last time I'll think of them. One thing is certain, I feel as though I was led to his grave for a reason. Maybe it was just to remember them, like they should be remembered.

Or maybe it was to help.

Either way, I'm happy this family found their way into my life. Heaven will take you, Captain Sibley. You just have to ask again. Rest in peace, my friend.

As for the cemetery and the land beneath it, the earth remembers and pays a solemn tribute to all the souls who walked upon it.

Joni Mayhan is a paranormal investigator and the author of 15 books, including *Bones in the Basement: Surviving the S.K. Pierce Haunted Victorian Mansion*. To learn more about Mayhan, please visit her website: JoniMayhan.com.

Chapter 2

DOGTOWN
GLOUCESTER
MOST HAUNTED: #12

"The trees are calling me near. I have to find out why. The gentle voices I hear ... draw me to going to the woods. I would hear the elders of the trees speaking to me. I often escape there in my dreams."
—*Murderer Peter Hodgkins reflects on Dogtown*

The first time I ever went to Dogtown I heard a lot of gunshots. It was the day after Thanksgiving and it was freezing cold out. There was no one in Dogtown that bright blue day except for me, my spouse, and our two friends. The trees had lost their leaves and we could clearly see stone walls and old cellar holes that would be hidden once the foliage returned again in the spring. It was magical.

Except for those gunshots. We had entered Dogtown near a firing range, and as we walked down the trail we could hear rifle shots echoing through the woods. We were alone, and someone was shooting guns nearby. It was unsettling.

I think those two words best describe Dogtown: magical and unsettling. Officially called Dogtown Common, this remote area is located between Gloucester and Rockport on Massachusetts's Cape Ann. Miles inland from the popular beaches and bustling towns, its 3,000 acres are filled with woods, swamps, huge boulders and a large reservoir. It's a vast expanse of rugged natural beauty.

Dogtown is an abandoned inland settlement on Cape Ann in Massachusetts. *Photo by Frank C. Grace.*

It's also an area with a long, strange history. Dogtown's woods are filled with the ruins of long abandoned houses. Its boulders are carved with unusual mottoes. A small marker commemorates a man's unusual death. Dogtown's history is one filled with witchcraft, decay, weird occurrences and maybe even a werewolf.

Sadly, Dogtown was also the site of a gruesome murder several decades ago. It happened on June 24, 1984 when schoolteacher Ann Natti was brutally killed by Peter Hodgkins. Natti had left her Gloucester home that morning to meet a friend in Rockport, and decided to walk there through Dogtown. Natti was unaware that she was being watched by Hodgkins, who was part of a long-established Gloucester family but had a history of psychiatric problems.

Hodgkins silently approached Natti from behind and pushed her to the ground. He then bludgeoned her in the head with a stone and pulled off her clothes. Suddenly realizing what he had done, Hodgkins fled the area in a panic, leaving Natti face down in the mud to die from her injuries. After her body was discovered Gloucester police quickly searched for Hodgkins, who had exposed himself to women in Dogtown in the past. Hodgkins was arrested on June 29, confessed to the crime, and was sentenced to life in prison without parole. It was a gruesome murder that shocked the Gloucester community, and colored people's perceptions of Dogtown for many years.

Hodgkins was interviewed in Elyssa East's *Dogtown: Death and Enchantment in a New England Ghost Town*. "Something calls to me," the murderer wrote in a letter to East. He said Dogtown had a significant effect on his life. "The trees are calling me near. I have to find out why. The gentle voices I hear ... draw me to going to the woods. I would hear the elders of the trees speaking to me. I often escape there in my dreams."

Dogtown's history started optimistically in 1721, when the leaders of Gloucester opened up the interior of Cape Ann for settlement. When the Cape had been settled in the early 1600s its center had been densely forested, but over time the trees had been cut down to make ships and buildings. This newly cleared area was dubbed the Commons Settlement.

Many new residents flocked to the Commons Settlement. The area was quite rocky and poorly suited to farming, but craftsmen established their workshops and homes there. Blacksmiths, millers and barrel makers plied their trades while sheep and cows grazed peacefully among the area's huge boulders. The people living in the Commons were known for their hard work and industry.

That all changed during the Revolutionary War. The population dwindled when the Commons men were called away to fight, and it grew even smaller when Gloucester's church was relocated. This might seem minor to a modern reader, but churches were an important part of Colonial life. The Commons Settlement was originally established near Gloucester's church, but the city's wealthier residents arranged for the church to be relocated closer to their waterfront homes. In just a few years the Commons Settlement had changed from a thriving village to an under-populated backwater.

A few people did remain in the Commons, mainly widows and other outcast women who took over its abandoned houses. Freed slaves also found refuge there. Packs of semi-feral dogs roamed through the village's streets, causing people in Gloucester to give it the derogatory nickname Dogtown. The name has stuck ever since.

Many of the Dogtown women survived by working as herbalists and fortune-tellers. For example, Rachel Rich foretold future events by looking at coffee grounds and sold a healing tonic made from foxberry leaves and spruce tops. Her daughter Becky earned her keep telling fortunes reading tea leaves, while another woman named Daffy Archer supposedly sold medicine made from snail mucus.

Naturally, these women developed a reputation as witches. It was a sinister reputation that some exploited for their own gain. Molly Jacobs worked as a fortune-teller, but also threatened to curse people who didn't give her money. Luce George did the same, but the most feared witch in Dogtown was her niece Thomazine 'Tammy' Younger.

Tammy Younger lived in a dilapidated house on the main road through Dogtown. Whenever she heard travelers approaching she would stick her head out her window and curse them with her baleful gaze (and her foul language). People gave her money, food or anything else she wanted to get her to reverse the curse.

Even after death she filled the people of Gloucester with fear. When she died in 1821 her nephew asked cabinet-maker John Hodgkins to make her a coffin. The Hodgkins family was used to having coffins in their home, but the witch's coffin filled Mrs. Hodgkins and her children with unnatural fear. Mrs. Hodgkins felt a strange chill, and thought it was caused by Tammy's spirit, even though the coffin was still empty. Only when the coffin was moved into the barn did the family rest easy.

By the 1830s Dogtown was almost completely abandoned and its last resident, a freed slave named Cornelius Finson, died in February 1839. Shortly before his death Finson was found by Gloucester's sheriff in the cellar of Molly Jacobs's empty house, digging in the frozen ground for buried treasure. Finson was half-starved and suffering from frostbite, so the sheriff brought him to Gloucester. He died a few days later.

Dogtown's reputation grew even more unsavory after this. Now a ghost town, its houses collapsed and its pasture became overgrown. People remembered it as a desolate village of witches, not as the hard-working Commons Settlement.

A sailor named James Merry added to the legend of Dogtown one night in 1891. He had recently traveled to Spain, and was regaling friends with tales of the bullfights he had seen. Someone mentioned a young bull they had seen in a meadow near Dogtown, and dared Merry to wrestle it. Merry was big, strong and vey drunk that night, so he agreed. The men walked to the meadow, where Merry successfully wrestled the animal to the ground.

Merry would be remembered as just another drunk if his story ended there. But it doesn't. One year later, on the night of September 10, 1892, Merry once again walked to the pasture to wrestle the same bull. This time he went alone and the bull, now hundreds of pounds heavier, gored him. His body was found in the meadow the following day. Merry's friends put up two small markers commemorating his battles with the bull, and they remain in Dogtown to this day.

The late Robert Ellis Cahill, a former Salem sheriff and collector of strange tales, wondered if something other than a bull might have killed Merry. The man was found with his throat slashed, which seems unusual for a bull attack. The moon was full the night Merry died. Could he have been killed by a werewolf?

The question sounds ridiculous, but Cahill explains his reasoning in a small book called *New England's Things That Go Bump in the Night*

Once a community settled by farmers, Dogtown was abandoned during the War of 1812. *Photo by Frank C. Grace.*

(1989). According to Cahill, the Native Americans who originally lived on Cape Ann said they were descended from dog-headed men. He also claimed they believed the wolfsbane plant transformed anyone who ate it into a wolf. For the record, wolfsbane is very poisonous so don't eat it. I haven't seen this folklore mentioned anywhere else, so I can't vouch for its authenticity.

However, a large mysterious animal has been seen in Dogtown for centuries. In 1879 a man named Amos Pillsbury saw a strange creature in the woods one night. Pillsbury said "its eyes were like fire coals, and it ran past me through the bushes … with every hair whistling like a bell." Pillsbury's grandmother had told him stories of this monster when he was young, but he doubted her until he saw it with his own eyes. A group of men searched the woods but the wolf-like creature was never found.

Was it the same creature sighted around Cape Ann in March of 1984? Some witnesses thought it might be a mountain lion, but the big cats have been extinct in Massachusetts for centuries. The creature was initially seen on a beach, but was last sighted on March 21 running down Gloucester's Raynard Street into Dogtown. It was described as a "gray monstrous dog-like animal … It had big teeth and was foaming at the mouth."

You can see why Dogtown has such a strange reputation, but in the 1930s the wealthy financier and Gloucester native Roger Babson tried to rehabilitate Dogtown's image. He hired unemployed masons to carve motivational slogans on its boulders. He hoped mottoes like *Be On Time*, *Get a Job* and *Help Mother* would remind visitors of the hard-working people who founded the Commons Settlement. The twenty-three carved boulders still remain, hidden in the dense forest, but I think visitors will find they just add to Dogtown's uncanny atmosphere.

These Dogtown legends have a certain spooky charm, and conjure up images of Massachusetts's historic past. In contrast, Ann Natti's murder was senseless and brutal. It's hard to reconcile the magical old folklore with the harshness of modern crime, but they exist side by side in New England. Bring a friend if you decide to explore Dogtown, because it's large, isolated and easy to get lost in. It's magical and unsettling, but sometimes there are scarier things in the woods than witches, werewolves and ghosts.

Peter Muise is a Boston-based author of *Legends and Lore of the North Shore* and founder of New England Folklore, the online hub for weird local news. To learn more about Muise, please visit his website: NewEnglandFolklore.com.

During the Great Depression, Roger Babson hired unemployed stonecutters to carve inspirational mottoes into boulders in Dogtown. *Photo by Frank C. Grace.*

Chapter 3

OLD SALEM JAIL
SALEM
MOST HAUNTED: #11

"Atrocities happened there, more so than executions, and they would kill each other in the prison because the conditions were so unbearable."
—Tim Maguire, Salem Night Tour

Salem's reportedly haunted correctional facility, which is believed to be the site of an estimated fifty hangings, has a long history of housing human monsters. Its lineup of usual suspects included Albert DeSalvo, more affectionately known as the Boston Strangler; hit man Joseph "The Animal" Barboza; former Mafia underboss Genaro Angiulo; and Brinks robber Joseph J. "Specs" O'Keefe.

Conditions in the old Salem Jail, which has oddly been refurbished into posh apartments, were notoriously horrific.

"It was a place that didn't have electricity or plumbing, even in the 1960s and 1970s," said Tim Maguire from the Salem Night Tour. "Atrocities happened there, more so than executions, and they would kill each other in the prison because the conditions were so unbearable."

The granite-walled jail and Federal-style keeper's house opened in 1813 next to the Howard Street Cemetery, where Giles Corey was crushed to death in 1692 over a torturous two-day period. The building was expanded in 1884, at which time its signature gothic, Victorian and

The old Salem jail, which opened in 1813, has been converted into a posh apartment complex. *Courtesy of the Boston Public Library.*

mosque cupolas were placed on the roof. The building's addition was constructed with Rockport granite salvaged from St. Peter Street near the exact spot where Corey was pressed to death. Some believed the rocks used to build the jail were soaked with blood from the 1692 witch trials executions.

Almost 100 years later, conditions were so awful inside—inmates still had to use chamber pots for bathrooms—that a few prisoners successfully sued the county because of its inhumane living conditions. When it closed in 1991 after a 177-year run as a county jail, the Essex County Correctional Institute or old Salem Jail was considered the oldest active penitentiary in the United States.

"We have left the dungeon behind us," said Essex County sheriff Charles H. Reardon at a ribbon-cutting ceremony for the new facility in Middleton in the 1990s.

But did they really? For more than a decade, the 31,630-square-foot jail ominously stood vacant. The boarded-up structure became a popular hot spot for vandals, and its historic facade started to look like a scene pulled from a Stephen King novel. It was during the '90s that the infamous correctional facility near the Howard Street Cemetery became the epicenter of Salem's ghost lore.

Based purely on aesthetics, the old Salem jail looked haunted.

"Many locals would go inside the jail and try to retrieve artifacts left behind," said tour guide Sarah-Frankie Clark. "It was common for people to see shadow people inside and even outside on the grounds. It was an extremely active location, and people talked about feeling a heaviness in the air. The conditions were really bad there, so I'm not surprised."

The riots at the old Salem jail were legendary. In July 1980, six inmates turned the facility into a sewer after dumping waste buckets on the floors at the institution. When the prisoners were evacuated from the pre–Civil War facility in '91, they "threw food, lit trash cans on fire and threw urine-filled buckets throughout the jail," reported the Salem Evening News. One inmate wrote "we won" in toothpaste on a table in the prison's rectory. According to another newspaper report on February 21, 1991, the mess included "pizza boxes, clothing and food thrown about the jail. Also, windows and televisions were smashed and several walls kicked in."

The building became a "magnet for vandals just one year after Essex County leaders vowed to give it to the city," reported the *Salem Evening News* on August 15, 1997. "The 185-year-old building had again been vandalized and some copper piping stolen from it."

It became a hangout for thrill-seeking locals during the late '90s. "Kids have been getting in there and it's become a party place," said Salem police captain Harold Blake in the '97 newspaper report. "Someone's going to be liable if anything happens there, and I hope it doesn't fall on the city."

As far as spirits, people regularly heard whispers and "metal-like" sounds echoing throughout the structure when it was abandoned. There was also a residual haunting of what appeared to be a prisoner holding a candle and walking from room to room…on a floor that no longer existed and had collapsed years prior.

The jail grounds were extremely active, and several locals claimed to have seen shadow figures and full-bodied apparitions of former prisoners darting across the yard and heading toward the chain-link fence as if they were making their great escape in the afterlife. Civil War soldiers, who were imprisoned in the old Salem jail, were seen wearing nineteenth-century clothing and moaning in agony from war-related punishments. In fact, several prisoners who spent time at the Essex County Correctional Institute said they shared a cell with long-gone inmates, or "residents" as they were called in the '80s, from the Civil War era.

One explanation for the onslaught of so-called spectral evidence from the abandoned structure was that the living were reportedly coexisting with the dead. Yes, the jail had squatters. "People have been living in there for nine years," said former public works director Stanley Bornstein in the October 15, 1999 edition of the *Salem Evening News*. "You patch one hole, they open another. Whatever you do, you're not going to keep people out of there. Somebody could easily be killed in there."

After the infamous penitentiary was turned into upscale condos and what was the sheriff's office became a popular St. Peter Street restaurant formerly called the Great Escape, A&B Burgers and now Bit Bar Salem, the dark shadows from its past seem to have taken a break. Perhaps their torturous sentence behind bars extended after death, and once the cellblocks were removed and the space was transformed, the correctional facility's invisible prisoners were finally set free. Or the old Salem Jail's squatters—both the living and their spirited roommates—found a new home.

For the record, Bit Bar Salem opened in the spot formerly occupied by the upscale restaurant known as the Great Escape and then A&B Salem. According to former tenant Amy Butler, she and her business partner found the perfect location for A&B Salem—even if it is haunted. "It would have ended up being a missed opportunity with it being the old jail," Butler told me. "It was vacant for thirteen years and the restaurant that was here before only lasted three years. Salem didn't really get a chance to hang out here and get the idea of what really went on here."

The granite-walled jail and Federal-style keeper's house opened in 1813 next to the Howard Street Cemetery, where Giles Corey was crushed to death during the witch trial hysteria in 1692. The jail was expanded in 1885 when two octagonal cupolas were constructed. Magician Harry Houdini staged an escape in 1906.

As far as the structure's ghost lore, Butler said she's heard several cautionary tales. "When we were purchasing the building, the previous owners told us a few ghost stories," she explained. "He said he would tell us a few but preferred not to tell us the others."

One encounter involved what looked like a figure wearing a dark shirt and pants, sporting an old-school cap and holding a clipboard. The previous owners initially witnessed this ghostly figure from a security camera. They thought he was a deliveryman until he disappeared in thin air.

"I have heard it was a janitorial gentleman with a set of keys and a period-dated hat," Butler said. However, it's believed that the figure is a residual haunting of a prison guard from the old jail's past. "When we were opening up this place, we definitely kept looking behind us," she continued. "There are spots in this building with freezing-cold air. I don't know what that means from a paranormal perspective, but it's cold in places where it shouldn't be cold. It's pitch black in the back. We try not to spend too much time there late at night."

For the record, these cold spots are signs of paranormal activity. In addition to the freezing patches of air, objects mysteriously break, and lights go on and off by themselves. "We have one employee who works in the back bar who constantly has the sensation that someone is breathing on her neck when no one is there," Butler said. "To be honest, the ghost stories kind of creep me out."

Then there is the ghost of Giles Corey, who supposedly unleashed his curse at the Howard Street Cemetery next to present-day Bit Bar Salem. "The rumor is if you see him, there is sudden death or heart-related death issues," she said. "I had a witch of Salem come up to the door and tell me if I see him, it's over."

Butler said she was wary looking out at the Howard Street Cemetery. "They say Giles appears in the windows of my building," she continued. "I had two women come who said they had an 'out of body' experience at the previous restaurant. They were attached to the table, shaking like crazy. I guess they were mediums, and they said they could feel the spirits in the building."

A&B Salem, which recently relocated to Beverly, moved out the old jail and Bit Bar Salem set up shop in early 2016.

Visitors to Bit Bar Salem's restaurant and arcade can get a ringside seat to Salem's most haunted cemetery. Opened next to the old Salem Jail, the spooky graveyard on a hill is the final resting spot for seafarer Benjamin Ropes, who was buried there on August 5, 1801. Cause of death? Ropes was fatally crushed while launching the historic ship *Belisarius*'s top mast. Oddly, a large percentage of those buried in the Howard Street Cemetery had a fate similar to Giles Corey, the only witch trial victim who suffered the "peine forte et dure" form of execution. Yep, a large percentage of those buried there were accidentally or purposefully crushed.

"We did some research with the city, and we found that a high number of the people buried in the Howard Street Cemetery, around 15 percent, were crushed to death," explained Maguire. "It's so interesting because that was the site where Giles Corey was crushed to death during the witch trials."

The Salem Night Tour owner rattled off a series of bizarre "accidents" of those buried at the Howard Street Cemetery. "For example, the floor of the jail collapsed and killed ten prisoners," he said. "A high number of people buried there were crushed to death because of various accidents."

Maguire was a featured player on the History Channel 2's documentary focusing on a handful of Salem's alleged haunts. The evidence he unveiled on the show, specifically a photo taken at the Howard Street Cemetery, was shocking. The picture looked like a crowd of Puritan-era revelers, gathered in a lynch mob sort of way, around what is believed to be the exact spot where Corey was stripped naked, placed under a wooden board and crushed to death over a two-day period in 1692.

"Someone on my tour took a photo of the cemetery," Maguire said on the History Channel. "By the end of the tour that person came forward to share the photo they took. Definitely not what we were looking at. There seems to be figures of people standing over someone. Most people who feel like they found the spirit of Giles Corey or have seen his apparition, they think it's a reminder of what we have done to him there."

Maguire told me that he rarely gives daytime tours. However, a Christian-based group requested an earlier time slot one day, and they snapped the infamous picture. "In the photo, you see what looks like flames in the background, and you can make out a couple of faces in the photo," he said, convinced he captured something paranormal. "When we were standing there, it was a nice, clear sunny day."

Over the years, Maguire said he's heard of multiple Corey sightings. "People often see an old man go around a tree in there. It seems to be the spirit of Giles Corey," he said, adding that the burial ground's proximity to the Old Salem Jail adds to its negative energy. "What's interesting about the Howard Street Cemetery is that it was built to accommodate inmate atrocities. It was the only coed jail in the country. Women were on one side, men on the other and children in the middle. There was a four-year-old boy who served a two-month sentence for breaking something."

It's common for visitors to report heart palpitations or a sensation of a heavy weight being placed on their upper body, just like the stubborn landowner who had rocks placed on his chest. It's also the norm for Salemites to mention Corey's curse.

"All of the Essex County sheriffs who overlooked that property eventually died of a heart-related ailment," said Maguire. "Robert Cahill (author of *Haunted Happenings* and sheriff who lived to seventy) was a firm believer in the curse. He had a bizarre blood ailment they couldn't diagnose. It's believed that Corey cursed the city and the sheriff in blood…and we have proof."

And if someone sees his apparition? Salem allegedly burns.

"My friend and I were exploring the Howard Street Cemetery," recalled Sarah-Frankie Carter on the History Channel. "There was a very creepy feeling as we got closer and closer to the spot where Giles Corey was actually pressed to death. My friend wiggled through a fence to see if she could get a closer look at the jail, and I heard her scream. She said she saw a man standing at the top of the stairs. We both had a really bad feeling."

Carter echoed the legend that if the "skeleton of Corey's ghost in tattered old clothes" appears, something horrible will happen to the city. "They say if you see Giles Corey, Salem burns. And if he speaks to you, you die," she said, adding that Salem did, in fact, go up in flames after her Corey sighting. "I was listening to my local college radio station, and they said there were fires in Salem. Needless to say, I don't go to that part of Salem anymore, especially at night. I don't think he gives you that many chances."

Locals believe in Corey's curse. In fact, author Nathaniel Hawthorne claimed that the apparition "of the wizard appears as a precursor to some great calamity impending over the community."

According to several accounts, Corey's spirit was spotted near the Howard Street Cemetery days before the Great Fire of 1914 that completely annihilated two-thirds of the city. Ironically, the inferno began in Gallows Hill, where nineteen innocents were hanged, and the conflagration destroyed one-third of Salem. "Before the Great Fire of 1914, there were almost three hundred accounts of local Salemites who had gone to the sheriff's office and reported this old man in raggedy clothes that they tried to help and then who vanished," confirmed Maguire, adding that he doesn't have solid proof of the lore. "They put enough stock into these accounts that the sheriff put deputies around the Howard Street Cemetery. They actually watched that cemetery for six or seven hours and when they had left, the Great Fire happened about a half-hour after."

Apparently, Corey's spirit continues to hold the city of Salem accountable.

Chapter 4

HARVARD UNIVERSITY
CAMBRIDGE
MOST HAUNTED: #10

"I wouldn't live in that house again for $1,000. It was enough to frighten people to death."

—Mary Nolan, witness to the Kirkland Street Nightmare

In 2014, I was interviewed by my friend Sarah Sweeney for the *Harvard Gazette* about the alleged hauntings lingering at the prestigious Ivy League college in Cambridge. "In my opinion, Memorial Hall is Harvard's most haunted," I told Sweeney. "Spirits have been seen looking out of the windows, and even walking the lawns outside the hall."

The article was published months after I was given an impromptu tour of the Annenberg dining complex within Memorial Hall. My first impression during the walkthrough? It looks like the Great Hall featured in the *Harry Potter* films. The structure, modelled after Christ Church in Oxford, features magnificent stained-glass windows by John La Farge, known for his work at Trinity Church in Boston, and glass from Tiffany's founder Louis Comfort Tiffany.

While looking from the upper level to the dining hall, I swear I spotted what looked like a young man trying to get my attention from across the hall. He was wearing period garb and disappeared after a second glance. I was told later that the spot where I saw the full-bodied apparition is Annenberg Hall's most paranormally active area.

One employee, who works in the historic building, believes there's an inexplicable energy, or a supernatural imprint, left on the space. "Sometimes it feels like somebody or something walks by and there's nobody there," he said. "It's like when somebody walks by and you feel the air move. Sometimes late at night, it feels like there is somebody standing behind you. It's so bizarre."

The source, who wishes to remain anonymous, said the area directly above Annenberg Hall's dining area is the building's most-active spot for alleged paranormal activity. "I like to think it was a former student, possibly one of the Civil War soldiers the building was built for," he said. "Because Annenberg Hall has always been a dining hall, it could be a chef or somebody who is in between worlds and is transitioning. I think the spirit is stuck and doesn't know which way to go," he said, adding that his friend who is a spiritualist confirmed that Memorial Hall is indeed haunted.

For several years, I produced a ghost tour called Cambridge Haunts and we had repeated sightings and hard-to-explain photos shot in the area believed to be Cambridge's haunted corridor. All of the guides on the ghost walk agreed Memorial Hall was the most active spot on the tour. "The building is electric and you can feel the energy when you're entering the pub," confirmed Hank Fay, a tour guide with Cambridge Haunts and local musician who regularly performed at the campus haunt. "When we're loading equipment in the area behind Queen's Head, the back of my hair stands up. There's definitely something strange going on in that building."

Another former tour guide, Rob Oftring, said he had an emotional connection with one of the tour's alleged spirits. The site is literally across the street from Memorial Hall. "Sam, I swear I saw Bertha standing in the yard on Kirkland Street," he told me, adding that he felt like the spirit had something to tell him.

Who's Bertha? According to published reports, she was believed to have been murdered in a house no longer standing on Kirkland Street across from Harvard's Memorial Hall. Human bones were found on the property but the victim was never identified.

Massachusetts Hall, the oldest surviving building on Harvard's campus, is home to a spooky tale about the ghost of Holbrook Smith, supposedly a member of the Class of 1914, though no record can be found of him. *Photo by Rob Oftring.*

Yes, Cambridge had its own version of *The Amityville Horror* known as the "Kirkland Street Nightmare." The Treadwell-Sparks House located at 21 Kirkland Street was originally built in 1838 and was moved from Quincy Street to its current location in 1968. However, the house that stood there before had a haunted history that made headlines in the *Boston Daily Globe* on April 8, 1878.

Over a fifteen-year span, tenants at the original house would come and go without giving any explanation. There were reports of disembodied voices, and after a series of revolving-door dwellers, the double-decker was abandoned for years because of its "haunted house" reputation. College students threw rocks through the windows, and stressed-out Harvard kids would squat at the dilapidated house for a spooky night out. In 1878, a man described as Mr. Marsh and his family rented the homestead for fifteen dollars a month and shrugged off the rumors that the house was haunted.

Soon, Marsh started hearing his name called out by a demonic, disembodied voice. He also watched in horror as the handle of his door slowly turned and opened when no one, at least among the living, was in the room. After close encounters with an unseen force, the man organized a Victorian-style séance. During the spiritual intervention, Marsh's wife allegedly became possessed by the so-called spirit haunting the house. Mrs. Marsh described in detail the story of an orphan girl who was forcibly taken into the home by a carriage where she was, according to the report, "foully dealt with, murdered and buried in the cellar below the house." During the séance, the spirit said her name was Bertha.

After a few months without paranormal activity, the house's freaked-out tenants started hearing odd noises in the home and up the stairs. They also heard the sounds of glass shattering in the kitchen, yet nothing was broken. The maid claimed she heard "terrible noises" at night and said the furniture in the room was pushed by invisible hands. She also recalled hearing blood-curdling shrieks and cries from a female voice.

After the initial article called "The Spook Roost" appeared in the *Globe*, former residents recalled seeing a full-bodied apparition of a young girl. They recounted objects, like plates on the kitchen table, moving when no one was there. Hundreds of curious spectators gathered around the Kirkland Street house at night while Mr. Marsh dug in the cellar to find the remains of the supposedly murdered girl known as Bertha.

Bones were found in the basement. However, a former tenant claimed that he would bury slaughtered animal bones in the cellar. Investigators couldn't tell if the remains were human or animal. In 1878, police didn't have the forensic and DNA tools investigators use today.

The Marshes, after undergoing public scrutiny because of the reports in the *Globe*, stopped talking to the press and demanded privacy. After several years, they fled the haunted house on Kirkland Street, and it was eventually demolished.

A former maid, Mary Nolan, confirmed the alleged haunting to the *Globe*. "Often I heard the carriage drive up, stop and then go on again. Why, that was quite common. We would hear the sound of wheels, the hoofs of the horses and sometimes the crack of the whip but nothing could be seen. I wouldn't live in that house again for $1,000," Nolan said. "It was enough to frighten people to death."

The late Reverend Peter Gomes, a prominent Harvard theologian and author who lived in the Treadwell-Sparks House until his passing, commented about the ghost lore surrounding Divinity Hall. The Kirkland Street house is near Harvard Divinity. "It was said that if you heard strange noises by the chapel or saw someone there you didn't recognize, it was probably a ghost," Gomes said, adding that the spirits were believed to be "benign, doubtless Unitarian, rational ghosts." Gomes never commented on the female spirit allegedly haunting his home on Kirkland Street.

William James—a Harvard luminary and founder of the American Society for Psychical Research, which is one of the oldest organizations exploring the paranormal—lived at 95 Irving Street, which is a stone's throw from the Kirkland Street haunt. His first essay for the society was about a girl who mysteriously vanished from her home in Enfield, New Hampshire. James investigated the haunting premonitions of Nellie Titus, who allegedly predicted how the sixteen-year-old died on Halloween in the late 1800s. According to the essay, Titus strongly believed that the girl drowned near a Shaker-style bridge in Enfield. Her body was found, but the case continues to be a mystery.

The dead girl's name? Bertha Huse.

Based on my first-hand experience, history and mystery lurk in just about every crimson corner at Cambridge's prestigious Ivy League. Harvard University is full of secrets, and its ghost lore reflects this centuries-old legacy of dead presidents and long-gone intelligentsia. Spine-chilling tales of unexplained sounds, phantom knocking and full-bodied apparitions have become a rite of passage for the uninitiated, college-bound progeny adapting to life in one of the Hogwarts-style halls scattered throughout Harvard Yard.

Elizabeth Tucker, a professor of English at Binghamton University and author of *Haunted Halls: Ghostlore of American College Campuses*, said that collegiate ghost stories are morality plays for the modern era. "They educate freshmen about how to live well in college," she explained in a 2007 interview, adding that the cautionary tales serve as spooky metaphors of fear, disorder and insanity. They also reflect students' interest in their college's historical legacy. Yep, campus ghost lore is a paranormal pep rally of sorts. "You don't find ghost stories at schools without a sense of pride," Tucker continued. "School spirits reflect school spirit."

The difference between Harvard's specters and other run-of-the-mill ghosts haunting universities throughout the country? Their spirits are wicked smart. Harvard's Massachusetts Hall has one respectable-looking student who returns every fall claiming to be a member of the class of 1914. Apparently, the residual apparition of Holbrook Smith never got the memo that he was kicked out of the Ivy League almost a century ago. There's also a Civil War–era apparition that allegedly haunts Memorial Hall. In 1929, a proctor reported seeing a man, who wasn't enrolled in the class, show up with a blue book in hand. The school spirit was known as the Memorial Hall ghost, and the "left behind" (a spirit that doesn't know he's dead) kept returning to class to finish the test—even though he died long ago.

Holden Chapel, which was used as the first cadaver room when the college hosted the Harvard Medical College, is rumored to be teeming with ghosts from its past. Built in 1744, the Colonial-style building was the spiritual gathering place as well as a secular lecture hall for Harvard students until 1772. The chapel housed 160 soldiers from 1775 to 1776 in the days leading up to the American Revolution. It later became the hub of Harvard's burgeoning medical school, established in 1783 by John Warren, and served as a morgue for students in training for half a century.

One legend alludes to Holden Chapel's macabre medical history. According to the late William C. "Burriss" Young, who lived in nearby Mass Hall as an assistant dean of freshmen, there's a female spirit that returns to Holden Chapel every year "around the first snowstorm."

Her name? Pickham.

According to Young, she was "a woman who was riding with her fiancé in a sleigh through the square when their horse slipped on the ice and their sleigh flipped over. Her fiancé broke his neck and died in her arms." According to the legend, he was buried at the Old Burying Ground, but "when she returned to visit the grave, the body had been dug up and stolen."

Back in the day, resurrection men—or grave robbers—would keep careful track of who died and where they were buried. When there was an opportunity to sell a body to a medical school, the resurrection man would go and dig up someone recently deceased. It was common practice for people like Ephraim Littlefield, who was a janitor at the Harvard Medical School and rumored to be a grave robber, to retrieve a dead body when the medical school's stock of cadavers was getting low.

The female spirit that allegedly haunts Holden Chapel "became convinced that her husband's body was in Holden Chapel, which housed the dissecting labs at that time," continued Young. "Every year, at the first snowstorm, she would escape from her family's house in New Bedford and try to break into Holden Chapel and would have to be physically restrained from entering. She's still spotted from time to time," Young told the *Crimson* in 1997. "And if you ever see her, and you observe carefully, you'll notice that she doesn't leave any footprints in the snow."

The medical school moved in the 1800s from Harvard Yard to Boston, where one of its famous alums, Dr. John White Webster, was accused of what was called the crime of the century: the murder of Dr. George Parkman. It's likely that Webster and Parkman made their first contact at Holden Chapel in the early nineteenth century.

Dr. Parkman was beaten and dismembered in a Harvard Medical College laboratory in 1849. Based on a bizarre plumbing accident that occurred on November 23, 1999, exactly 150 years after Parkman's macabre murder, his spirit is rumored to haunt the house that bears his family name. It faces the Boston Common and is located at 33 Beacon Street. Also, the Parkman Bandstand, located in the center of the public park and erected posthumously, stands as a solemn reminder of one of the most talked about trials of the 1800s.

It's a tale of a $400 loan turned deadly.

Hailing from one of the most prominent families in Boston, Parkman was a retired doctor who became a landlord and moneylender in the early 1800s. Nicknamed "old chin," Parkman befriended one of his clients, John White Webster, who was a professor of chemistry and geology at Harvard Medical College. Incidentally, the Parkman family donated a large sum of money to fund the Harvard's medical school's move to Boston from its former location near the Mass General Hospital.

Webster borrowed $400 from Parkman, who was reported missing days following an attempt to collect his money. Bostonians were on the hunt for the missing landlord, and police printed twenty-eight thousand missing-person fliers. After a sensational trial and Webster's eventual confession, the press had a field day spitting out "Harvard Professor and Murderer" headlines guaranteed to captivate the city. On August 30, 1850, the professor was hanged at the gallows.

How did Webster murder Parkman? After an unexpected collections call at Webster's laboratory, the professor took his walking stick and clubbed Parkman in the head during a momentary fit of rage. Panicked, Webster reportedly chopped up the body into pieces and threw the remains into the privy, also known as a toilet.

In his confession, Webster claimed that it was an act of self-defense. He said that Parkman "was speaking and gesticulating in the most violent and menacing manner" about the loan. In response, Webster "seized whatever thing was handiest—it was a stick of wood—and dealt him an instantaneous blow with all the force that passion could give it. It was on the side of his head, and there was nothing to break the force of the blow. He fell instantly upon the pavement. There was no second blow. He did not move."

During the trial, a police officer testified that Parkman's torso was found in a bloodstained tea chest, which was displayed to the court. Webster also allegedly burned Parkman's bones, including his jawbone replete with false teeth, in the furnace. The officer also said that it was possible to fit the victim's remaining body parts in the toilet, but the torso wouldn't fit.

With such a macabre legacy, Holden Chapel today looks like a throwback to Harvard's days of yore. For most of the twentieth century, it hosted the Harvard Glee Club and later the Radcliffe Choral Society. The chapel was renovated in 1999, and archaeologists discovered human remains in the building's basement. "My first thought was, 'Oooohh, an old Harvard murder,'" said Associate Professor of Anthropology Carole A.S. Mandryk in a 1999 *Crimson* interview. "They're definitely human bones." According to the report, workers found several sawed-open skeletons, broken scientific glassware and test tubes strewn among the remains. "Between 1782 and 1850, part of the basement was used as an anatomy and dissection lecture hall for the Medical School," wrote the *Crimson*. "Some of the bones have metal pieces sticking out of them, as if someone was trying to construct a skeleton," Mandryk added.

Remember the wailing female spirit known as Pickham that returns to Holden Chapel during the first snowstorm? She hasn't been spotted since the building's renovations. It's possible that she was right and her husband's remains were buried in the basement. Perhaps Pickham finally got some postmortem closure when the bones were unearthed and removed from Holden Chapel.

Chapter 5

CASTLE ISLAND
SOUTH BOSTON
MOST HAUNTED: #9

"The enlisted men were outraged, and as they dug Massie's grave they quietly plotted how to avenge his death."

—*Peter Muise, New England Folklore*

Edgar Allan Poe had a love-hate relationship with his hometown. The author, who notoriously didn't like Boston, was born in the Bay Village and died in Baltimore, at age forty, in October 1849. In the late 1980s, a local cab driver and Poe enthusiast was dead set on marking the spot where Poe was born. He decided to create a bronze plaque, made it himself and bolted it to the building now occupied by the not-so-scary burrito joint Boloco on the corner of Boylston Street and Charles Street South across from Boston Common. The plaque says it was placed by the Edgar Allan Poe Memorial Committee, which has only one member—the acerbic cab driver.

While Baltimore, his final resting place, seems to have claimed him as its own, Boston has embraced its "Poe-ness" and erected a memorial statue, unveiling it in October 2014, around the corner from his birthplace. The square has become a major attraction honoring the author of "The Raven" and "The Tell-Tale Heart."

Boston-born author Edgar Allan Poe was honored with a commemorative statue on the corner of Boylston Street across from the Boston Common. *Photo by Sam Baltrusis.*

Poe was born in Boston on January 19, 1809. The offspring of two actors, the young Poe was sent to Virginia after his mother died and his father abandoned him.

He returned to the city of his birth in 1827 under financial duress. By the age of eighteen, Poe had amassed a considerable gambling debt. To raise funds and avoid his debt collectors, he joined the army under the fake name "Edgar A. Perry." Because he was too young to enlist, Poe lied and said he was twenty-two years old. Much to his chagrin, the soon-to-be-author's regiment was sent to Boston.

Poe was stationed at Fort Independence on South Boston's Castle Island. While he reportedly wasn't happy with the homecoming, the Boston Harbor fort might have been inspiration for one of Poe's most popular stories.

According to Peter Muise, author of *Legends and Lore of the North Shore*, Poe was looking for inspiration. "One day Poe noticed a gravestone in the fort's cemetery for a Lt. Robert Massie, who had died on December 25, 1817," Muise recalled. After Poe commented on the misfortune of dying on a holiday, one of his fellow soldiers told him the tragic story behind Massie's death."

Massie was well liked by his peers at Fort Independence. However, one of his fellow officers, Gustavus Drane, had it in for the new recruit. Drane, an expert swordsman, argued with Massie over a card game on Christmas Eve. Drane challenged him to a duel and killed Massie on December 25, 1817.

"The enlisted men were outraged, and as they dug Massie's grave they quietly plotted how to avenge his death," continued Muise. "A few nights after the duel they put their plan into action. First, they invited Drane to come drink with them. Once he was heavily inebriated they led him to an unused alcove inside the fort and chained him inside. Finally, they walled up the alcove with bricks, sealing Drane inside forever."

According to lore, Poe was inspired by this real-life gruesome tale of revenge. Poe was discharged from Fort Independence in 1829, and the buried-alive story involving Drane was believed to be inspiration for his 1846 classic *The Cask of Amontillado*, in which a man takes revenge on his drunken friend over an insult and ultimately entombs him alive.

Is the legend true? Muise said Poe did serve at Fort Independence, but there is some debate about what really happened between Massie and Drane. A plaque at Fort Independence supposedly inspired Poe to dig for the backstory. Massie's remains were moved from Boston and reburied in Fort Devens. "It does appear that Massie was actually killed by Drane, but his killer was not entombed alive," continued Muise. "Instead Drane avoided a court martial, moved to Philadelphia, and got married. He died in 1846 at the age of 57."

However, a crew of Brown University archaeologists did find the remains of two charred human skeletons in the early 1900s. Also, folklorist Edward Rowe Snow claimed that a skeleton wearing a military uniform buried in the bowels of Fort Independence was found in 1905.

In The Islands of Boston Harbor, Snow also wrote that Castle Island was cursed. According to pre–Revolutionary War legend, an English gentleman lived on the island with his daughter. The daughter had two suitors: One was British and had been picked by her father, and the other was a colonist. She was smitten with the American boy, and the British man, enraged, challenged his competition to a duel. The Brit won, killing the young local. In a true Romeo and Juliet twist, the girl is said to have committed suicide in response to her lover's death. "The British officer, heartbroken, rushed down to the dock and plunged into the channel, crying he would put a curse on all who ever came near the island," wrote Snow. "Some sailors still believe that many shipwrecks near the Castle are to be blamed on this curse."

Snow said Castle Island was known for its bizarre suicides, including a man who jumped to his death in 1903 and a Somerville man who shot himself in the head in one of Fort Independence's casemates.

Castle Island is also known for its sea serpent sightings. "They were seen in 1819, 1839 and 1931," added Muise. "There were a lot of sea serpent sightings off the North Shore, particularly in the nineteenth century, but sadly only a few have been seen in the Harbor. Maybe it was just too busy or too polluted to sustain giant sea monsters?"

As far as Edgar Allan Poe's ghost is concerned, it's said that the Bostonian opted to haunt his former home in New York City's West Village. The 85 West Third Street location was where Poe penned the final draft to his classic *The Raven* as well as *The Cask of the Amontillado*.

New York University's Furman Hall has taken over the historic West Third Street location. The three-story building where Poe lived for eight months from 1844 to 1845 was torn down in 2001.

All that remains is the façade of his former brownstone and what some say is the Boston-bred icon's ghost. There's a lamppost in front of the allegedly haunted structure and according to the website *Curbed*, "Poe's ghost has been seen climbing it by spooked law students."

Has his ghost been spotted recently? According to multiple sources the answer is, well, "nevermore." Maybe the literary icon's spirit has returned to Boston?

Chapter 6

METROPOLITAN STATE HOSPITAL
WALTHAM
MOST HAUNTED: #8

"It sounds like it came straight out of a horror film ... except it's true."
—Laura Giuliano, paranormal investigator with Para-Boston

I don't do asylums. But here I am, walking through what's left of the Metropolitan State Hospital in Waltham. The former psychiatric facility opened in 1930 and quickly earned a not-so-stellar reputation for its sadistic, overcrowded conditions. The hospital's Gaebler Children Center, for example, reportedly medicated the children to an extreme and, based on local legend, resulted in multiple fatalities.

And then there was the heinous "hospital of the seven teeth" homicide. In 1978, Anna Marie Davee was murdered by co-patient, Melvin Wilson. He dismembered her body and buried pieces of the corpse in several shallow graves scattered on the grounds of Met State. Wilson also kept seven of Davee's teeth which he tucked away as sociopathic souvenirs. Two years after the murder on August 12, 1980, Wilson escorted police on a sick-and-twisted tour of the hospital's grounds showing police where he buried pieces of Davee's dismembered body.

It should be no surprise, but it's said that *American Horror Story: Asylum* was inspired in part by Met State's dark, mental-patient past.

Laura Giuliano, an investigator with Para-Boston and Met State regular, warned me about the haunted crime scene that has been converted into a luxury apartment complex. She believes there is evidence of a potential cover up at the former asylum. "It sounds like it came straight out of a horror film ... except it's true," Giuliano told me.

"Can you imagine a 57-year-old man who has been in mental facilities since he was 17 having complete access to a 36-year-old woman who has been in mental facilities half her life? Based on the facts of the case, he was freely traipsing around the woods on the grounds of the hospital property and had the time to make a hut, kill this poor woman, have access to a hatchet, cut her up into pieces, pull out seven of her teeth, bury her in three holes and return to his room with seven of her teeth," Giuliano said.

"If that is not horrific enough, Met State hospital employees noticed Miss Davee was missing," she emoted. "The next day they decided to look for her. They found a hut, clothes and bed linens in the woods, and within a day they disassembled the hut and washed the linens," Giuliano continued, adding that it's a "sad and sick story on so many levels."

When I first started writing historical-based ghost books back in 2011, I swore I would stay far away from the horrors that unfolded in the series of former asylums scattered throughout Massachusetts. The two that terrified me the most were Met State and Danvers State Hospital. Ironically, both former hospitals have been renovated by the present-day owners of my apartment at AVA Somerville. It's a rental community known as Avalon Bay. As an empath, the lingering energy was too much for me to handle.

I somehow pick up on the negative fingerprints left behind at the various locations I visit during the research phase of my books. The trauma of the thousands who lived and died at these inhumane institutions has somehow psychically imprinted itself into the environment. If I go to the former asylums, I believed, I would relive the pain. In a worse-case scenario, one of the lost souls would follow me home. Based on first-hand experience, some tortured attachments are nearly impossible to shake.

Since the hospital's closing, the area to the west of where the buildings once stood has been developed into apartment housing. *Photo by Jason Baker.*

Human monsters were created in asylums. A murderous entity hitching a ride with me was the last thing I needed. In fact, the idea terrified me.

In 2012, I was interviewed by my former colleague, Scott Kearnan, from the *Boston Phoenix* when my first book, *Ghosts of Boston: Haunts of the Hub*, was released. I had no problem talking about the theories of potential stay-behind spirits based on my experience, but refused to actually go to these extremely haunted asylums. No way.

"Based on the intense residual energy at many of the former mental institutions scattered throughout Massachusetts, it would make sense that many of the people who lived in these buildings left behind a psychic imprint of sorts ... especially if there was neglect or trauma involved," I told Kearnan. "The hypothesis developed in the 1970s, known as the Stone Tape theory, speculates that the environment can absorb energy from a high-tension event, like a lobotomy or suicide, and the theory is a possible explanation for alleged paranormal activity like lights flickering or inexplicable screams reported at the insane asylums in the Boston area."

I wanted to believe that the hauntings at the former institutions were purely residual. In fact, my response to Kearnan kept reiterating the concept of a videotaped event that played over and over. "Residual spirits are not intelligent entities, or poltergeists, and can't interact with the living," I continued. "However, it's possible that a few lost souls still linger where they lived which happened to be a mental institution for thousands of unfortunate people."

Based on evidence found by Giuliano and her team, my professional opinion has changed. "We investigated inside one of the renovated Met State buildings in April of 2013. We set up in the lobby of the building and there was a gymnasium on the floor above us that we did not have access to," she said. "About an hour after beginning the investigation, our lead investigator was listing with headphones and something captured his attention. He didn't want to say what it was, but instead passed the headset around for us all to hear. Everyone agreed it was clearly the sound of children singing. It was creepy singing, though. Not like an upbeat song, but a slow, eerie song like *Ring Around the Rosie*. We couldn't make out their words but it was extremely unsettling," Giuliano told me.

In 1978, Metropolitan State patient Anne Marie Davee was murdered by another patient, Melvin W. Wilson. *Photo by Jason Baker.*

According to reports from the early 1960s, more than two dozen children died and were buried on the grounds. It is said that they were poisoned by strontium that doctors were adding to their milk, believing that it was a way to treat their mental illness. According to Giuliano and Para-Boston's case reports, the ghosts of these children are said to still haunt the property. "Interestingly, it was after the investigation that we learned of the urban legend that sometime in the 1960s two dozen children allegedly died from poisoning," she explained. "Because we were in a basement lobby at night with an auditorium and gymnasium above us with open access to all members, we could not unequivocally say we were hearing the spirits."

Ghost children singing *Ring Around the Rosie*? I'm convinced. Believe it or not, Giuliano has uncovered even more creepy evidence from this haunted location. "Months prior to our investigation, I wandered around the 330-acres of Met State," Giuliano recalled. "In a dense area, on the slope of a hill, I found the foundation of a small shack. Under many decades of composting leaves and brush something white caught my eye. It was a sheet. I uncovered it and it said "Property of Metropolitan State Hospital." I couldn't believe it. A foot or two away I found an old, outdated pair of brown women's leather shoes. The area was covered in poison ivy so I took pictures and carefully ripped off the part of the sheet that contained the words of the hospital and took it home with me."

Giuliano said it's important to her respect the victims from Met State's blood-stained past. "I have covered over the area and I've never taken anyone to it because if this was the area that Davee was murdered, I don't want her to endure any further desecration or disrespect," she said.

Based on the paranormal investigator's first-hand encounters, does she believe it's haunted? "If I hadn't heard the creepy singing of children with my own ears I would not be so confident. Our investigation took place years after the condos were built and we heard the singing," she said. "The employees that use the basement level have told me their paranormal stories and I've heard stories from folks living in the new condos."

Giuliano continued: "Something is going on there. I hope it is just unexplainable energy caught in time and not spirits unable to move on."

Chapter 7

HAWTHORNE COVE MARINA
SALEM
MOST HAUNTED: #7

"There was one incident that really messed with him. It creeped him out so much he didn't want to talk about it."

—John Denley, Boneyard Productions

Salem doesn't want to be the next Spooky World. At least, that's what local haunter John Denley, known in the haunted-house business as Professor Nightmare, was told when he set up shop in the city a few decades ago.

Over the years, he's had his hand in a lot of the city's scare tactics, including Terror on the Wharf and the current Witch Mansion on Essex and Escape Room Salem on Church Street. His consulting business, Boneyard Productions, helps clients around the world create spooky spaces, and he currently has an office in the city. Denley, who helped build Witches Woods, Spooky World and Madison Scare Garden, said he's seen a backlash in Salem against the traditional haunter business.

"Salem would rather bury its history than embrace it," Denley said. "From my experience, Salem is indicative of the supernatural, but there's a push to focus on its maritime history. People don't come to Salem for its maritime history. They come here to be scared."

In response, Salem set up a bevy of "museums" to educate visitors, including the Witch Dungeon Museum and the Salem Witch Museum, while offering a few scares along the way.

One of Denley's tales from the crypt involves a salty sea captain spirit who yells, "Get out of here." It's this disembodied voice in the dark that spooked the late Robert Ellis Cahill, noted author of *Haunted Happenings* and a prolific folklorist responsible for putting a twist on much of Salem's storied ghost lore.

"When I knew Bob, his thing was about debunking a lot of the supposed hauntings in Salem," recalled John Denley, founder of *Fright Times* magazine and long-time mastermind behind several haunted houses in Salem. "People all over the city called him to check to see if their houses were haunted. However, there was one incident that really messed with him. It creeped him out so much he didn't want to talk about it."

The site? A two-story structure built by sea captain Herbert Miller from a salvaged barge at Hawthorne Cove Marina near the House of the Seven Gables. During the summer, the marina is the hub of Salem's seaside activity. During the colder months, the location—formerly known as Miller's Wharf—is a virtual graveyard of winterized vessels with boats wrapped in protective tarps. There's also an ominous "private property" sign and a black dog that protects the two-story structure, which served as a "fish-food restaurant" back in the day. Cahill's friend Mike Purcell purchased the dwelling and said the previous owner recycled the hull of a barge and hoisted it up to create a second floor to what was his summer cottage. The building was rumored to have an odd energy to it, but Purcell couldn't figure out why, so he called Cahill. After some research, it turned out that the hull of the two-story structure was potentially a crime scene of a savagely butchered sea captain.

Cahill didn't know much about the location in the '80s before hearing the voice that haunted him for years. It was a disembodied growl that came from nowhere: "Get out of here." Cahill described it as a "raspy, gurgling voice," and it spoke to him twice.

"There was no one else in the room and the voice had that eerie quality of coming from beyond the grave," wrote Cahill in New England's *Ghostly Haunts*. "I felt the heat of anxiety flood my face and body, but I didn't move."

Cahill was convinced the recycled barge was haunted but didn't know the history of the building when he published *Ghostly Haunts* in 1984.

Hawthorne Cove Marina, formerly known as Miller's Wharf, reportedly has a negative energy of a murdered sea captain. *Photo by Andrew Warburton.*

He called Herbert Miller's daughter, but she had no clue. It was years later that the barge's possibly back story emerged, and it was more gruesome that Cahill could have imagined.

After years of research at the Salem Public Library, Cahill uncovered some shocking history that possibly linked the haunted barge to a horrific murder in 1911. It's speculated that the salvaged vessel was possibly a barge called the *Glendower*, whose captain, Charles Wyman, was bludgeoned to death with an axe. He was whacked twenty-seven times according to the February 7, 1912 edition of the *Boston Daily Globe*. "Capt. Wyman was found lying face downward in his bunk. He was dead," reported the Globe. "His face and head were covered with cuts and bruises. Blood stains were on the walls and ceiling of the cabin, although there was no sign of a struggle."

Members of the crew, including an old Norwegian deckhand named Bill Nelson, were not covered in blood, and the murder became a "who done it?" of sorts. An investigation by the Boston police found that William De Graff, the Glendower's hunchback cook, was possibly the murderer. One crew member testified that De Graff said that "Captain Wyman is no good," and the captain was axed to death at about 2:00 p.m., right after lunch. Prosecutors didn't have convincing evidence linking De Graff to the crime, and he was found not guilty thanks to the defense of noted attorney John Feeney. After the trial, the cook disappeared and was never heard from again. However, it's still believed the Dutch hunchback was indeed the culprit.

One spine-tingling piece of testimony echoes Cahill's haunted encounter at Miller's Wharf. According to the *Glendower*'s deckhand Nelson, he heard a muffled scream come from the captain's cabin around the time of the murder. Wyman's ominous last words according to Nelson's testimony? "Get out of here," he recalled.

Two years after the trial, a Philadelphia-based seaman claimed the Wyman murder was revenge. "De Graff had specifically gone to Newburyport from Philadelphia to join the Glendower crew as cook, for the sole purpose of murdering Captain Wyman," said John Breen during an investigation in 1913. Apparently, Wyman had assaulted De Graff earlier in his career. "Wyman had physically flogged a young seaman out of the ship's rigging in a rage, causing him to fall to the deck, crippling him for life," Breen recalled. "The seaman was De Graff."

Cahill retold the story of the *Glendower* in his book *Haunted Ships of the North Atlantic* in 1997. During a public speaking event at Purcell's restaurant, a Salem-based surveyor, responsible for measuring the property around the wharf, approached Cahill and told him he had heard a similar disembodied voice growl those infamous four words: "Get out of here." Cahill was convinced. Mystery solved.

However, was the *Glendower*'s crime-scene hull truly used as Herbert Miller's summer cottage? After doing some research on the Wyman murder, I uncovered a series of newspaper clippings from the 1911 murder. There's one shot of jury members from the De Graff trial, wearing turn-of-the-century garb, walking the deck of the ill-fated barge. Oddly, the pilothouse does look very similar to the current structure at Hawthorne Cove Marina.

"The barge, because of its horrid history, never went to sea again," wrote Cahill in *Haunted Ships*. "I think it was the barge that Herbert Miller purchased for pittance, towed to his wharf in Salem, some 12 miles away, and winched up to make a second story for his summer home. It is, I believe, the spirit of Captain Charles Wyman that haunts Miller's Wharf. His final words, shouted at the hunchback when he entered the captain's cabin with a concealed axe, are forever on his lips."

Chapter 8

COMMERCIAL STREET
PROVINCETOWN
MOST HAUNTED: #6

"If a person loved a location so much they didn't want to leave it, even after death, they often take offense when those living there decide to make changes."
—Joni Mayhan, author and paranormal investigator

On All Hallow's Eve, Provincetown's Commercial Street was abuzz with both the living ... and the dead. I was on a walking tour with ghost host Jeffrey Doucette, a former colleague at Haunted Boston and co-founder of Haunted Ptown, a tour I helped produce. As Doucette and I crept through the dark alleys of the town, revelers paraded up and down the main drag.

"The weather has been a horror show," said Doucette, a veteran tour guide known for his over-the-top theatrics and spine-tingling delivery. He was dressed in a tuxedo, holding a lantern and sporting a skull face-paint job. "Look at 'em," he said with a smile. "The freaks are out tonight." He pointed at the crews of scantily clad trick-or-treaters showing off their costumes.

Compared to Salem on Halloween, Provincetown's fearsome phantoms constructed the most elaborate and creative costumes I've ever seen.

A vampiric-looking man was standing in front of Whaler's Wharf with pointy ears and fangs, showing off his "Cape Cod Casket Co." coffin. He looked like an adult version of Eddie Munster. He playfully hissed and

Take a stroll along Provincetown's Commercial Street where the historic Lancy mansion is allegedly haunted by an old woman who died in the late 1800s, but due to the frozen ground, she couldn't be buried, so her son kept her propped up at an open window all winter long. *Photo by Sam Baltrusis.*

posed for a picture. A flock of fractured fairy-tale fairies were wearing green tutus and granting make-believe wishes with magic wands.

There was one figure sitting on a bench dressed like a "bat boy." He was hiding in the shadows as passersby admired his expertly crafted costume. Looking closely, his eyes were red and the fur covering his face looked extremely authentic. I was genuinely creeped out.

"You've seen the movie *Jeepers Creepers*, right?" mused Doucette. "Well, Provincetown has its own boogie man. He's known as the Black Flash."

According to legend, a grim reaper type beast was known to snatch children away. The cryptid made national headlines. When the phantom of Provincetown was first reported in the 1930s, some locals were suspicious that the creature had arrived around Halloween.

Surely it was just a prank, right? Not according to reports.

Dressed in a black cape, the monster appeared to have bat wings and was known to suddenly drop into a visitor's path from a tree or rooftop. "He was all black with eyes like balls of flame," claimed one man in a 1930s-era newspaper account. "And he was big, maybe eight feet tall. He made a sound, a loud buzzing sound, like a June bug on a hot day, only louder."

One boy claimed that "it jumped out" at him from nowhere "and spit blue flames" in his face. Alleged sightings of the Black Flash continued for a decade. One townie, who found his dog barking at the demon, claimed he shot it. However, he said that the Flash dodged his bullets and continued to laugh maniacally. The creature then leaped over the man's backyard fence.

The Black Flash made its last appearance in the mid-1940s when it supposedly chased a family home. As they gathered inside, one of the school-aged children doused the creature with a bucket of water—similar to what Dorothy did to the Wicked Witch in *The Wizard of Oz*. It's not been seen since.

Or has it?

"He's known to come out on Halloween," continued Doucette. "But I think it's just an old legend to keep the kiddies from staying out too late."

After the Haunted Ptown tour, I returned to the bench where I spotted the furry cryptid earlier. He was gone. What was odd about the costume is that its head was way too small compared to the rest of its body. And his perfectly crafted bat wings. Man, they were so authentic. And, like in Doucette's story, his eyes were red, "like balls of flame."

I walked up and down Commercial Street looking for the *Mothman Prophecies* lookalike. No luck. Like the legend, he was gone in a flash.

Adam Berry, formerly from *Ghost Hunters* and a year-round resident, said that you can't throw a rock down Commercial Street, the town's main drag, without hitting a haunted hot spot. "You're looking at one of the oldest places on the Cape. Yes, it's haunted," he said. "Provincetown is where the Pilgrims first landed. It's where they set up shop. It has to be haunted," said Berry, who co-founded the Provincetown Paranormal Research Society (PPRS) with his partner Ben Griessmeyer in 2006. "If you think about all of the shipwrecks in Provincetown, Wellfleet and Truro, there's got to be something here."

Berry swears that Provincetown's town hall is chock-full of ghosts. "It used to be an old jail and the people who work there say that the offices downstairs are haunted," Berry said, adding that the town hall's former jail once housed Marlon Brando who spent the night in the drunk tank after playing bongos on the street. "I don't have proof but people say that it's active. During construction employees claimed that tools and ladders were moved by an unseen force and that you could hear disembodied voices, which makes sense because construction usually brings up activity."

The original town hall was on High Pole Hill at the present site of the Pilgrim Monument. It was destroyed by fire on February 16, 1877. The current structure was built in 1880 and cost around $50,000 to build.

"For years, town hall's basement served as Provincetown's jail. Not intended for long-term prisoners, the cells in the basement were quintessential 'pokey' where many revelers, who were too drunk to find their way home, spent the night to 'sleep it off,'" confirmed *Provincetown Magazine*. "Those cells, which held the likes of Marlon Brando and Eugene O'Neill, were preserved during the renovations. The bars and bricks are nicely incorporated into the town's building department office."

According to the team from Manchester Paranormal Investigations in New Hampshire, the first question they ask when people contact them about an alleged haunting is whether the location has recently been renovated. "A spirit may or may not like the changes being made to his or her environment. One thing to remember is a spirit who has remained behind has some anchors that makes them bound or choose to remain in this realm," explained the investigative team. "Sometimes the spirit likes to remain in a comfortable environment since oftentimes a spirit may be confused, angry or in a poor state of mind. When their familiar surrounding becomes a bit chaotic, as is often the case with renovations, they become a bit uncomfortable. For those that do not realize they are dead, suddenly their surroundings are changing without explanation."
Spirits unhappy with the changes to a historic location will meddle with construction, like moving ladders or causing objects like paint brushes or power tools to disappear.

Joni Mayhan, a paranormal researcher and author of *Bones in the Basement* and *Devil's Toy Box*, told *me* that the two-year, $6 million renovation project to town hall from 2008 to 2010 could have conjured up activity. "Yes, it's not unusual for a construction project to stir up paranormal activity that might have previously been dormant," Mayhan explained. "I see this frequently in older houses and buildings. If a person loved a location so much they didn't want to leave it, even after death, they often take offense when those living there decide to make changes."

Mayhan said she has first-hand experience with spirits making a postmortem protest against a renovation project. "We gutted the basement of our first house, removing an old work bench that had obviously been used for decades by someone who had lived in the house before us," she continued. "Not long afterwards, we began hearing footsteps in empty rooms and began seeing shadows move that had no explanation. I've seen it happen over and over again with others, as well. Sometimes the dead don't mind sharing our space, but they aren't always happy when we decide to alter it from the way it once was."

Veteran tour guide Doucette said town workers are still creeped out about the structure's basement. "While inquiring about permitting, I was directed to speak with one of the departments down in the basement," Doucette recalled. "For a period of time, the basement held the town jail.

It's rumored to be haunted. During my conversation with someone within the permits office, a woman who worked in the building interrupted my conversation and said, 'I don't know what's down here, but I don't like being down here alone. It creeps me out.'"

When Doucette asked her why the space scared her, she sheepishly explained: "I always feel like there is someone down here with me."

So, who or what is haunting the basement of Town Hall? No one knows for sure. However, paranormal experts suggest that it's likely someone who died unexpectedly when the jail served as a drunk tank. Someone like Zeke Cabal, who was known for his drunken shenanigans in the 1920s, could have left a psychic imprint of sorts on the location.

Or, if big names pique your interest, it could be *On The Waterfront* icon and legendary bad boy, Marlon Brando, playing his bongos in the afterlife. He spent one helluva night in the makeshift jail. Yes, he could be a contender.

A few blocks down Commercial Street from Town Hall was the former home to Provincetown's very own Norman Bates. Built by Benjamin R. Lancy Sr. for his mother in the late 1880s, the mansion was designed to emulate a Beacon Hill brownstone and towers over Commercial Street behind Cortile Gallery at 230 Commercial St.

"Opposite the remnants of Lancy's Wharf behind Colonial Cold Storage is a magnificently eccentric Second Empire pile built in 1874 for Benjamin Lancy, a merchant and ship owner," reported the Provincetown Historical Commission, noting that the aesthetically creepy structure has an *Addams Family* vibe to it. "After Lancy Jr. died in 1923, the building was acquired by the Research Club, a history-minded civic group, to be used as the historical museum."

According to the Historical Commission online, the Lancy family was notorious for its eccentricity. "Local legend credits his father, also Benjamin Lancy, with refusing to allow Commercial Street to be laid out in a straight line in the West End," continued the report.

Lancy's approach to building the creepy mansion was just as odd as his public persona. The house was designed "using a process which he had discovered and invented to finish wood so that it resembled the then-fashionable brownstone," reported the *Advocate*. "With this method of treating wood he hoped to make a fortune, and although he did manage to accumulate a sizeable amount of money, none of it came from his discovery."

Apparently, the house was "considered ugly," wrote the *Advocate*. However, "in time, people softened toward it."

The mother, known as "Grandma Lancy" or Nabby by the locals, wanted the tallest house in Provincetown, reported the newspaper, but "died before it was completed."

The woman specifically asked her son for a "widow's watch," or a cupola, so she could "keep account of the goings and comings of all ships in the harbor," as well as a bird's-eye view of the neighbors, reported historian and family descendent Louise Holbrook in the *Advocate*. "Lancy found an old ship's carpenter repairing ship's stairs in one of the Lancy's vessels. It was the only kind of stairs he ever built. So he built ship's stairs in the cupola of the Lancy mansion," she added.

The beloved Nabby passed on February 27, 1896. However, the macabre part of the story isn't the way the old matriarch died but what happened to her after her death.

Lancy kept his dead mother in the house for months "because a grave could not be dug in the frozen ground," Holbrook explained. "When spring came the body was still in the upstairs front bedroom … until the neighbors complained. Family tradition relates that due to public pressure they finally buried their beloved mother three months after her death."

According to a letter from her great-great-granddaughter, the windows were kept open to chill the room and to keep the stench of death out of the house.

Six months after his mother's passing, Lancy's opera-singing wife had had enough and left the momma's boy. She returned to her wealthy family in Providence, Rhode Island. Mr. Lancy's son, reportedly even more eccentric than his father, inherited the house.

The strange habits of the Lancy men became Provincetown legend. "He was used to going swimming when he felt like it, sans bathing trunks," Holbrook wrote. "Even when he was an old man, he would come out of his Lancy mansion, walk straight down to the water, take off his clothes and swim nude. But no one paid any attention in 1912."

For the record, there was nothing between the mansion and the Provincetown Harbor "but a sandy front yard to Lancy's own wharf, for he owned a small fleet of ships—some for fishing and some for cargo."

Lancy Jr. became a recluse, known to collect horse dung for heating fuel. "He closed the house with its pretentious furnishings, and together with his sister, moved into the basement where they lived in miserly frugality," reported the *Cape-Cod Standard Times*. Lore suggested that the spirits inhabiting the 20-room, brownstone-looking structure drove Lancy Jr. mad.

Passersby have spotted the apparition of a lady in black peeking out of the mansion's upstairs front bedroom and cupola. It's the spot where Lancy Sr. propped up his dead mother during the winter as they patiently waited for the cemetery's ground to thaw.

Jeannie Dougherty and Charles MacPherson, two former tenants who shared the top floor apartment at the Lancy Mansion in the 1990s, said they spent many sleepless nights in the creepy house. "They often witnessed lights turning on and off seemingly of their own volition. On one occasion, a hairdryer, which was put away in the closet, turned on by itself," reported *Cape Encounters*. "One afternoon when Charles was alone in the apartment he saw in the bathroom mirror somebody walking by behind him."

Dougherty, who roomed above the mansard roof near the staircase leading up to the widow's watch, said she heard phantom footsteps, implying a residual haunting, leading up to her room. "I literally froze in terror as I heard footsteps come straight up my stairs toward my bedroom door and then stop," she said. "I was too afraid to leave my room, but I can assure you I had every light on in the room that night and didn't sleep."

There's significance to the hairdryer mysteriously turning on in the closet.

Visitors, specifically women, who have visited the art gallery beneath the Lancy Mansion, claim to have felt the sensation of their hair being touched. Some even say they felt as if their locks were being brushed or groomed by an unseen force.

Adding to the tale from the crypt, after her death Lancy would brush his mother's hair, chatting with her as if she was still alive. Letters from family members confirmed the tale, claiming that Lancy combed the decaying woman's hair and even cut her nails.

Chapter 9

FREETOWN STATE FOREST
BRIDGEWATER TRIANGLE
MOST HAUNTED: #5

"If you were a victim, I don't know how you would escape the clutches of a murderer out there. It seems like the forest could swallow you ... and it has to."
—Rachel Hoffman, PXP's "True Crime Paranormal"

The so-called Bridgewater Triangle, an area of about 200 square miles in Southeastern Massachusetts, is an epicenter of the Commonwealth's alleged paranormal activity and over-the-top urban legends. Tales associated with the Triangle include: Native American curses; satanic cults; a red-headed hitchhiker; a swamp called Hockomock, which the Wampanoag tribe believed was "the place where spirits dwell"; numerous UFO sightings, including one as far back as 1760; three-foot cryptids known as Pukwudgies; and the Assonet Ledge in Freetown State Forest, where visitors report seeing ghosts standing, jumping and inexplicably disappearing.

Of all of the hocus pocus occurring on the spooky South Coast, the most spine-tingling story about the Bridgewater Triangle is the real-life horror that unfolded in Freetown State Forest in November 1978. The decomposed body of Mary Lou Arruda, a teen cheerleader from nearby Raynham, was discovered tied to a tree in the forest. The murdered girl was 15 years old. She disappeared in the afternoon of Sept. 8, 1978. A newspaper delivery boy found her bicycle near the scene. She was missing for two months.

James M. Kater, a 32-year-old donut maker from Brockton, was indicted in connection with the Arruda murder. His green car was spotted in Raynham and his vehicle had a nine-inch gash in the front that matched the girl's bicycle. He was also on probation for a similar incident in 1968 when he kidnapped a girl from Andover. Kater has stood trial four times and his final appeal was rejected by the U.S. Supreme Court in 2007. He is currently serving his sentence in federal prison in California.

According to trial documents, "Arruda had been alive and in a standing position when she was tied to the tree." Once she became unconscious, the weight of her head against the ligature around her neck caused her to suffocate. While there are no ties to her murder and the alleged reports of satanic cult activity in Freetown State Forest, the case reinforced the idea that the area is cursed.

"The Town of Freetown was purchased in 1659 from the Wampanoag Tribe and the town was incorporated in 1683. The Native Americans believed the land was highly sacred when Wamsutta sold it, possibly without the backing of the tribe, maybe the cause of the evil energy," reported the SouthCoast Ghost paranormal group online. "Many believe that events of the area have turned the once gentle spirits violent, attracting evil to it and the forest in return is being fed by the evil. Native Americans claim the horrible crimes and hauntings will not stop until the tribe is given back the land."

People who stumble on the location where Arruda's body was found say it's paranormally active. "I have seen shadow people," reported an anonymous paranormal investigator on the *Unexplained Mysteries* forum. "I have seen a spirit of a girl near the site where they found Mary Lou Arruda's body in 1978. I recently spent the entire night in the forest with my group. We had some people feel like they were pushed. We heard laughter in the woods. Occasionally we heard groans, breathing and screams." The source reported seeing lights like softball-sized fireflies at the top of the trees. "One from our group swore she saw someone jumping from tree to tree but it was unverified."

Another source on *Unexplained Mysteries* echoed claims about the negative energy associated with the forest. "I had the distinct feeling we were being followed and watched," he confirmed. "I could have sworn I saw people in the woods."

Assonet Ledge in Freetown State Forest is where visitors report seeing ghosts standing, jumping and inexplicably disappearing. *Photo by Frank C. Grace.*

One year after the Arruda murder, all hell broke loose in the cursed Freetown State Forest. Karen Marsden, a woman believed to be a prostitute in Fall River, was savagely murdered. Carl Drew, a self-proclaimed devil worshipper and pimp, supposedly led ritualistic gatherings in the forest at a place known as the Ice Shack. The so-called "son of Satan" was also accused of three cult-like murders.

"Drew was on trial for the February 1980 murder of Karen Marsden, a Fall River prostitute whose skull and other remains were found in a wooded area of Westport in April the same year," reported *SouthCoast Today*. "While on trial for Marsden's murder, he was also under indictment for the October 1979 killing of Doreen Levesque, another Fall River prostitute."

Robin Murphy, an 18-year-old sex worker who was granted immunity to testify against Drew, claimed the man organized at least 10 satanic gatherings, which led to three ritualistic murders. "At the trial, Murphy said that she, Drew and two others had driven Marsden to a wooded area of Westport where they got out of the car and Murphy began dragging Marsden through the woods by her throat and hair," explained *SouthCoast Today*. "Drew told Marsden to give Murphy a ring she was wearing but she refused so Drew cut her finger off to get it."

Murphy, who claimed to have been possessed by Satan, said she slit Marsden's throat because the cult leader demanded it. Murphy testified that Drew carved an "X" in the murdered woman's chest and started speaking in a demonic tongue. He then dabbed the mutilated woman's blood on his fingers and marked an "X" on Murphy's forehead, telling her that the sacrifice was an initiation into his cult. Murphy said two other murders, including the savage slaughter of Levesque, were eerily similar.

Séances using the skulls of the victims were supposedly held, according to Murphy, in the Freetown State Forest. "The killing of Doreen Levesque was an offering of the soul to Satan and so was the killing of Miss Marsden," Murphy said to the court. Drew is still in prison for the three murders he was accused of inciting 25 years ago.

Inspired by the Drew case, Freetown State Forest became a hotbed of black mass gatherings in the '80s. One man, William LaFrance was found camping in the forest with rows of yellow candles and satanic symbols carved in the dirt. Officers found "666" tacked to the tree near LaFrance's car. Park rangers claimed that the haunted Assonet Ledge was also plagued with freshly painted satanic symbols, skulls and pentagrams in the late '80s. For the record, visitors still claim to encounter spirits at the abandoned quarry, which is believed to be the site of multiple suicides over the years.

The ranger station, a cabin-like structure built in the 1940s for loggers in the forest, is where a lot of the cult activity is believed to have taken place. People who claimed to have seen the wooden structure said it's where Carl Drew held his infamous drug-induced séances. Animal bones have been found in the area near the hijacked shack. There's also a structure known as the "Ice Shack" but it's commonly mistaken for the ranger station.

Located five minutes from Fall River and Taunton, the extremely haunted Freetown State Forest is located in the lower-right corner of the Bridgewater Triangle. *Photo by Frank C. Grace.*

There was also a bunker in the Freetown State Forest. Rangers found pentagrams and evidence of ritualistic gatherings in the culvert-style cave. Officers believed the bunker was evil. However, former members of the Society of Creative Anachronism (SCA) claimed it was a gathering spot for neo-pagan and Wiccan practitioners and not followers of the devil.

In addition to all the alleged cult activity, a ghostly trucker has been spotted regularly on Copicut Road in the heart of Freetown State Forest. He supposedly blares his horn and threatens passing motorists who venture into the forest at night.

There's a site called Profile Rock that looks like a man's face carved in a granite outcropping. Lore suggested that it was the face of the great Native American sachem, Chief Massasoit, leader of the Wampanoag people. He's responsible for saving the Pilgrims in Plymouth from starvation by offering corn to the dying settlers.

Whether Freetown State Forest is actually haunted or not, there's no denying it's freakishly macabre history. As someone who has spent time in the forest, there's definitely an eerie electricity that permeates the 5,217-acre area. There was a massive fire in the woods in March 1976 that damaged 500 acres and another in September 1980 that destroyed 230 acres.

In addition to the murders in the late '70s, more deaths occurred, including that of a drifter who was killed in 1987 after being mistaken as an undercover police officer. Two men were shot to death on Bell Rock Road in 2001 and there were two assaults in 1991 and 1998.

Rachel Hoffman and Tina Storer produced a documentary on Freetown in 2014 for their *True Crime Paranormal* series. The ghost-hunting team said the serene forest turned nightmarish after dark. The Bay State's most haunted forest? Both investigators believe the Freetown State Forest is a hotbed of primordial evil. It's almost as if the forest somehow devours its victims.

"The negative energy this place is well known for makes you so susceptible to energy being sucked out of you," explained Storer.

Hoffman agreed. "It wasn't hard for us to see how bodies could be hidden for three to six months at a time," Hoffman continued. "The forest is extremely dense and the drop offs are extremely high. The highway goes in all different directions. If you were a victim, I don't know how you would escape the clutches of a murderer out there. It seems like the forest could swallow you ... and it has to."

But is it haunted? Absolutely. It's as if the Freetown State Forest has a devilish mind of its own.

Chapter 10

GARDNER-PINGREE HOUSE
SALEM
MOST HAUNTED: #4

"Of all of the places we visit, we get the most photographic evidence from the Gardner-Pingree House."

—Tim Maguire, Salem Night Tour

It's arguably Salem's crime of the century. The murder of Captain Joseph White, an eighty-two-year-old shipmaster and trader, riveted the nation in 1830 and inspired literary giants like Edgar Allan Poe and Nathaniel Hawthorne.

The crime scene, a three-story brick mansion built in 1804 and located at 128 Essex Street, is believed to boast a residual haunting, a psychic imprint of sorts replaying the savage murder of White, who was whacked over the head with a twenty-two-inch piece of refurbished hickory, also known as an "Indian club," and stabbed thirteen times near his heart. According to several reports, a full-bodied apparition peeks out of the second-floor window. A female spirit rumored to be White's niece, Mary Beckford, who served as his housekeeper in addition to being his next of kin, is also said to haunt the Essex Street house. Beckford's daughter, also a Mary, was formerly part of the household in the 1820s but moved to Wenham with her husband, Joseph Jenkins Knapp Jr.

Every major city has one: a murder house. In Salem, it's known as the Gardner-Pingree estate.

The Gardner-Pingree House, 128 Essex Street, allegedly contains an anniversary haunting of the murder of Captain Joseph White, an eighty-two-year-old shipbuilder. *Photo by Frank C. Grace.*

"There were two guys from Oregon who came here to debunk things and they captured on video what seems to be a man looking out of the window," recalled Tim Maguire from the Salem Night Tour. "Of all of the places we visit, we get the most photographic evidence from the Gardner-Pingree House. I've been inside the house a few times and I feel more of a presence of a woman. There's definitely a female presence there."

Maguire says Salem's murder house is one of many haunted crime scenes scattered throughout the Witch City. "There's an energy here that's different. I feel it a lot stronger in Salem than say Boston," he said. "A lot of places like Gettysburg and the Bermuda Triangle, there tends to be electrical issues. Salem has an electrical fault under the city. People who visit here notice that their cellphones drain fast. There are electrical oddities that were noticed by the Native Americans in 1618. They considered it a spiritual place and thought it was odd that Europeans wanted to stay in Salem."

Maguire said these electrical anomalies explain why Salem is supposedly a hotbed for the paranormal. "The Native Americans talked about seeing things here … or feeling a presence here," he continued. "When I'm doing a paranormal investigation in Salem, I have to let people know that when they put their meter on the ground they're going to pick up stuff because Salem has an electrical issue."

Psychic imprint from the past? Paranormal investigators like Adam Berry formerly from *Ghost Hunters* believe that residual energy associated with heinous crimes, specifically murders, has potential to leave a supernatural imprint. "Anytime there's a traumatic event, it could be left behind," Berry said. "If you walk into a room and two people have been arguing, fiercely, you can feel that weirdness that they've created or energy they emit spewing at each other. I do think there's a form of energy that can be left behind from a traumatic event or any kind of murder or suicide in a room. The theory is that maybe that energy goes into the walls and lingers there."

As far as the murder, it's a complicated puzzle that has been twisted over the years. Captain White's grand nephew, Joe Knapp, learned that the retired merchant had just completed his will, leaving $15,000 to Mrs. Beckford. Knapp believed if White died without a will, his mother-in-law would inherit half his fortune of $200,000. So, Knapp and his brother John hired a black sheep from the respected Crowninshield family, Richard, to slay the captain in his sleep for a mere $1,000. Knapp had access to White's Essex Street home, and in April 1830, he stole the will and left the back parlor window unlocked. Beckford and her daughter Mary were staying in Wenham.

Richard Crowninshield slipped into the mansion at night "entering the house, stealthily threaded the staircase, softly opened the chamber door of the sleeping old man." He killed him with a single blow to the left temple, according to an account in the April 1830 edition of the Salem Observer. Crowninshield hid the murder weapons under the steps at the former Howard Street meetinghouse. The bludgeon, a hickory-stick club, was "fashioned to inflict a deadly blow with the least danger of breaking the skin. The handle was contrived as to yield a firm grasp to the hand."

Because of its witch trials past, Salem is considered to be one of New England's most haunted destinations. *Photo by Frank C. Grace.*

As far as the crime scene, White was in his bedchamber lying diagonally across the bed on his right side. Blood oozed from the thirteen stab wounds and oddly, no valuables in the house were missing. Because there was no theft, police detectives were baffled at first. The Knapp brothers falsely claimed they had been robbed by three men en route to Wenham, which added some initial confusion to the murder mystery.

A gang of assassins in Salem? Yes, there were three, but it was the Knapp brothers and murder-for-hire crony Richard Crowninshield, who later hanged himself with a handkerchief tied to the bars of his prison cell before he was convicted. The Knapp brothers were then put on trial after the prison suicide.

Daniel Webster, giving arguably one of his most famous legal orations, served as the Knapps's prosecutor and called the affair "a most extraordinary case" and a "cool, calculating, moneymaking murder." The Knapp brothers, admitting they had planned the crime and fabricated the robbery story, were convicted. Meanwhile, it's believed that Edgar Allan Poe was inspired by Webster's speech and penned "The Tell-Tale Heart," a classic short story involving the guilt and retribution associated with the grisly murder of an older man. Hawthorne was also entranced by the trial and explored similar themes in *The Scarlet Letter* and *The House of the Seven Gables*.

Thousands gathered in downtown Salem to watch their public executions. John Francis Knapp was hanged on September 28, 1830, in front of a blood-soaked haunt from Salem's past: the former Witch Gaol, or witch dungeon, currently located at 10 Federal Street. His brother Joe, considered to be the mastermind behind the crime, met a similar fate three months later in November. The infamous murder weapon, the custom-made "Indian club" that measures more than twenty-two inches, is owned by the Peabody Essex Museum. Unfortunately, the macabre artifact isn't on display today, but visitors can tour the refurbished mansion.

According to several reports, the historic murder repeats itself spectrally on the anniversary of Captain White's death. There are also many sightings of a male phantom, believed to be White, gazing out of the second floor of the Gardner-Pingree House as the living frolic up and down Essex Street. If White's spirit truly has a calendar, his next scheduled appearance is April 6.

As for the city's penchant for historical coincidences also known as the "Salem factor," the family home of White's murderer, the Crowninshield-Bentley House, was literally moved next to the crime scene in 1959. Yep, the murderer's house was placed next-door to the murder house. Sometimes fact is stranger than fiction.

Chapter 11

ORLEANS WATERFRONT INN
CAPE COD
MOST HAUNTED: #3

"My wife says don't upset the ghosts. We look at it as Hannah's inn. It's her home and we take care of it for her."
—Ed Maas, Orleans Waterfront Inn co-owner

I'm doing an overnight at the allegedly haunted Orleans Waterfront Inn on July Fourth weekend in Cape Cod. Oddly, the fireworks are happening inside this historic structure built in 1875. I somehow chose the haunted spot, which is Room 5. Unbeknownst to me at the time, my bed for the night made a recent cameo on an episode of Syfy's *Ghost Hunters*.

"Built in 1875 the inn was initially a hardware store and then renovated into a speakeasy run by the Irish mob, as well as a bordello," reported MassLive in a recap of the 2010 TAPS investigation. "There was a murder on the premises. One of the prostitutes was found dead outside of the inn. Various other apparitions were reported including two of the workers who committed suicide, both by hanging, on the premises and a naked woman dancing in the lobby."

I purposely don't do research before going to a supposedly haunted location. When I booked the hotel, I liked the room's name which is simply "1875," a hat tip to the year it was built. Of course, I chose the suite where guests check in but refuse to check out. Yes, according to reports there were two women who were "not right" and refused to leave on their own accord. Employees at the inn claimed that they would hear

It was only after purchasing the property that Ed Maas discovered that the Orleans Waterfront Inn was haunted. *Photo by Sam Baltrusis.*

what sounded like an animal growling and possibly a foreign language that sounded like German when one woman barricaded herself in the second-floor locale.

"We are also told about the history of Room 5 where not one but two women checked in for a weekend and then stayed for about five months only being removed forcefully from the rooms, one by family, one by the police," reported MassLive.

Owner Ed Maas, who purchased in the haunted hotel in 1996, wrote about the room in his book *Ghost of the Orleans Inn*. He believes it's related to a reported suicide from a German visitor in the inn's downstairs bathroom. "Although the cause of death may have been determined, it is unclear of the manner. If it was by knife was the owner of it perhaps escorted away from the scene? There is little information about the death and little is ever spoken of it," Maas wrote. "The room above the restroom is particularly interesting. Guests check in for a short stay and seem unwilling to leave. One particular guest exhibited multiple personalities as a German SS soldier. To hear the German cursing coming from the elderly female was frightening. It seemed as if German interrogations were going on behind closed doors."

Within the first hour of my stay, I chatted with the owner's daughter, Meaghan, who gave me a brief walk-through of the location that has been featured on Syfy's *Ghost Hunters* and various paranormal books. In the lobby, there is a "hidden room" that housed bootlegged liquor and other underworld activities during its Irish mobster-era heydey. Meaghan told me about the history of my room and recounted how two previous guests refused to leave. "It's definitely a room with a strange history," she joked, struggling to unlock the door. "You should definitely visit the cupola upstairs before it gets dark."

Within the first hour, I went to the top floor and read a letter to "Hannah," the resident spirit of the 1875 inn. I carried an iOvilus with me as I walked through the hotel's belvedere and then
creeped up into the cupola. The air in the small room overlooking Orleans's Town Cove felt psychically charged, as if something horrible happened there. With the iOvilus, I picked up "with" when I asked if the spirit was with us. It also said "Jones" and "devil" when I asked who murdered the inn's resident ghost.

I had an intense reaction in the cupola, as if the spirit in the room wanted to communicate with me. It was a male energy and words like "rubber" and "sex" kept coming up on the spirit box. The novelty investigation tool was spewing words so fast, I had to turn it off. The spirit seemed sexually charged, and somewhat misogynistic. I didn't know it at the time, but the cupola is where the bartender, Fred, hanged himself in the 1950s.

The cupola is also where Steve Gonsalves from *Ghost Hunters* picked up an EVP that sounded like "let me out." However, Gonsalves believed it said "get me down."

Mark Jasper wrote about the Orleans Waterfront Inn in *Haunted Cape Cod*. The chapter is appropriately called *Gangsters & Ghosts*. "The house was originally built in 1875 by Aaron Snow II for his wife and seven children. He was a direct descendant of Constance Hopkins, who was the first person to spot Cape Cod from the Mayflower as it sailed near Eastham in 1620," Jasper wrote. "Hannah and Fred are thought to be the two ghosts responsible for some of the bizarre incidents that have transpired in the inn over the years. Unsure of the identities of the murdered prostitutes, the Maases named the female ghost Hannah. Fred, you recall, was the bartender who hanged himself in the cupola. Hannah apparently loves to play with doors."

She also apparently loves to play with paranormal researchers. My overnight stay in this extremely haunted hotel was terrifyingly memorable. When I was sitting on the bed and reaching for my computer, I felt something rub up against my leg. I told my partner about the bizarre sensation. It turns out the inn has a history of "ghost cats," specifically in the neighboring Room 4.

I also captured an EVP outside of the inn that still haunts me. I was sitting on a bench near the 300-year-old Jonathan Young windmill and I had what I can only explain as a psychic moment reliving what I believe to be the murder of the young woman who still lingers in the inn. Based on my vision, she was in love with one of her suitors and he shot her because she knew too much. I have no idea what the vision means, except that she was completely not expecting to be shot outside of the structure known as "Aaron's Folly" by a man she was courting.

During the EVP session, I asked the spirit if she was murdered. I picked up what sounded like a whispering female that got progressively louder as the recording continued. When I asked her to tell me her name, I clearly picked up what sounded like either "Anna" or "Hannah." I was in shock. I quickly packed up my stuff and moved inside. I would have probably left the haunted Orleans Inn after that eerie EVP session. However, I was scheduled to interview the owner the following morning.

One of the first things Ed Maas heard from the locals after he purchased the historic Orleans Waterfront Inn in 1996 is that the property is notoriously haunted and it's in his best interest not to upset the ghosts.

When asked if he knew the Orleans Inn was haunted before he purchased it, Maas shook his head. "I had no idea," he told me. "I had driven by the inn for 25 years and never came inside. It was slated to be knocked down and I wasn't told by the realtor. After we purchased it, I then found out that the inn was written about in the *Cape Cod Times* and I called the realtor and asked them about it and I quickly learned the inn was rumored to be haunted. We then made ourselves comfortable with the ghosts."

Maas initially shrugged off the spirited stories until he had a face-to-face encounter with the female apparition of a ghost he now calls Hannah. "When we bought the inn, I would stay here around the clock. At midnight I would lie on the couch to get some sleep. In the middle of the night, I saw what I thought was one of the guests come downstairs stark naked and I said 'hello' and she 'hello' back. I didn't think much of it until a woman stopped her car outside of the inn a few days later after she saw a naked woman dancing in the fifth floor belvedere. That's when I put two and two together."

The owner said he had the initial encounter with Hannah in 2000. When I asked him if he has had any experiences with the ghosts outside of the property, he quickly told me that is where she was killed. "Hannah was murdered outside," he explained. "We believe she lived in Room 5, but most of the sightings have been in Room 4. In fact, we just had a group record an EVP session with Hannah and they asked her if she was happy and she said she was. During the Roaring Twenties, this was a house of ill-repute. We believe the spirit is the woman who was murdered here in the 1920s."

Maas, the father of eight children, said his family is at peace with the inn's resident spirits. "We don't tell the guests about the ghosts before they check in," he continued. "Some people know about it and some come here specifically for the hauntings. It's not something that we really promote. My wife says don't upset the ghosts. We look at it as Hannah's inn. It's her home and we take care of it for her."

Chapter 12

USS SALEM
QUINCY
MOST HAUNTED: #2

"I could see them through the curtain and two of the girls had scratches all up and down their legs ... and they were bleeding."
—Kim Mello, volunteer with the USS Salem

The Sea Witch smells like death. "It's the paint," joked one of the volunteers who greeted me as I clumsily stumbled onboard the historic *USS Salem* in Quincy. "There were hundreds of dead bodies on here during the earthquake in Greece in 1953 and many of them died from burns ... so that could explain the peculiar smell as well."

One of the first things I was told when I reported for duty as the manager of the VIP paranormal experience on Ghost Ship Harbor, a new haunted attraction slotted for the *USS Salem* during the 2016 Halloween season, was not to disrespect the ghosts.

While it's not a typical crime scene compared to the other haunts featured in this book, the *USS Salem* has seen more death than your average Naval vessel. What's also unique about this haunted location is that the crimes committed on this ship are allegedly perpetrated by the ghosts. Yes, the Sea Witch's spirits are out for blood.

Launched on March 25, 1947, in Fore River Shipyard in Quincy and nicknamed the Sea Witch by her crew thanks to a three-month stint in the so-called witch city, the *USS Salem* never saw combat but was certainly a harbinger of death. In fact, the area beneath her mess hall became a makeshift morgue during the previously mentioned earthquake off the coast of Greece in 1953 and it's estimated that at least 400 dead bodies

The *USS Salem* is home to a new haunted attraction called Ghost Ship Harbor in October. *Photo by Frank C. Grace.*

were kept on the vessel. According to additional reports, at least 23 babies were born on the ship during the 1950s.

The USS Salem is a heavy-metal celebrity of sorts. She made a cameo in the action-packed thriller from Disney called The Finest Hours starring Casey Affleck and Chris Pine. The vessel was also featured in a film called the Pursuit of the Graf Spee in 1956. And, of course, the haunted vessel was featured on Ghost Hunters a few years ago.

It should be no surprise but it's the ghost ship's alleged paranormal activity that generates the most regional buzz.

The USS Salem's volunteers, a motley crew of former military veterans and lovers of the Des Moines-class heavy cruiser, spewed off a laundry list of resident ghosts including "The Burning Man," who also smells like death and reportedly hides in the berthing area beneath the third mess hall where the bodies were kept during the Ionian earthquake, a ghost kid who speaks Greek, a salty sea captain, a growling devil dog, a cook who likes to keep the kitchen in order and a man named John who reportedly gives tours of the USS Salem in the afterlife.

There's also an angry sentinel spirit known to get aggressive if you disrespect the Sea Witch.

Kim Mello, a long-time volunteer on the ship and former manager of the *USS Salem's* haunted house, told me about a group of teen-girl haunters who were banging on the freezers in the wardroom pantry. "I told them to stop disrespecting the spirits but they wouldn't listen," she said, describing the former haunter scene full of living dolls. "I could see them through the curtain and two of the girls had scratches all up and down their legs ... and they were bleeding. I know they didn't do it to themselves because I was watching the whole thing as it happened."

Mello said the mysterious scratches were mere "love marks" compared to the nightmare her team of volunteer haunters endured when they were told to move the haunted house off of the ship. In 2013, access to the vessel was shut down because the MBTA deemed the wharf was unstable. In addition to hosting paranormal investigation teams and overnight visits for Boy Scout groups, the heavy cruiser had a 20-year run as the U.S. Naval Shipbuilding Museum in Quincy and served as a symbol of the city's shipbuilding history during the 1940s.

"It was a nightmare," Mello said, referring to the volunteer group's attempt to resurrect the ship's haunted attraction. "We had a circus freak show theme and we had a tough time keeping the tents up during the season. Plus, it was freezing."

Jason Egan, the hauntrepreneur behind Fright Dome in Las Vegas and mastermind behind the new attraction onboard the *USS Salem*, had an equally rough ride in his search for the ideal location to produce a Boston-area attraction. Egan and local marketing guru Matt DiRoberto were swatted down twice when they tried to unleash their initial vision called Fright Island on Georges Island and then Castle Island in South Boston.

Egan's dream of creating his world-class haunt on a Boston Harbor island was ultimately squashed. However, he and DiRoberto approached the *USS Salem* and they were eager to create an attraction on a notoriously haunted location.

Paranormal Xpedition's Rachel Hoffman has heard a crying baby in the medical area. The tables with stirrups were used as facilities for childbirth. *Photo by Frank C. Grace.*

"We kind of fell into this location. Originally we were gearing for an island but then we came across this ship. This thing is huge and it's actually haunted. I'm very excited to launch this haunted attraction in such a unique and iconic location," said Fright Dome owner Jason Egan. "Over the years, my team has created some of the top Halloween events in the world, from Las Vegas to Hong Kong. To launch in a new market like Boston and work in a location that is notoriously haunted is amazing."

Rachel Hoffman, an investigator with Paranormal Xpeditions and one of the handful of experts working with me on Ghost Ship Harbor, said her team uncovered a lot of activity in the hospital unit. "We heard a crying baby in the medical area," she said, adding that there are tables with stirrups indicating facilities for childbirth. In the so-called "butter room" or "meat locker where the bodies were kept while at sea was the thickest, most active area," Hoffman told me in an interview for my book 13 Most Haunted in Massachusetts, adding that her team heard banging and that others reported being touched when no one else was onboard.

The USS Salem also boasts a few misogynistic spirits who frequently retaliated when Hoffman's all-female crew investigated the ship. For the record, the vessel was decommissioned in 1959 and its alleged spirits reflect the sentiment prevalent during the World War II era. "The most active was the admiral's quarters where we got EVPs," she continued. "The men didn't like ladies on their ship. I think the ghosts of the men who served still reside with their old-school rules." Paranormal Xpeditions also picked up an electromagnetic voice phenomenon, or EVP, of what sounded like a pig on the top deck.

The USS Salem's proverbial ghost cat was let out of the bag in October 2009 when Syfy's Ghost Hunters investigated the 718-foot cruiser.

In the anchor windlass room, Condon told the The Atlantic Paranormal Society (TAPS) team that "one of our volunteers, his name was John, used to work in this space, maintaining and cleaning it. One day he passed away and we noticed people saying they met this terrific tour guide named John," the vessel's executive director Michael Condon said, adding that they didn't have any tour guides on the ship at that time. "He's very active in this spot and people actively see him and even talk to him."

The *USS Salem*'s archivist, John Connors, told *Ghost Hunters* he'd heard phantom footsteps above him on the main deck when he was working ... and no one else was aboard. *Photo by Frank C. Grace.*

Tom Ventosi, a volunteer with the *USS Salem*, said he saw a woman in white in the restricted medical area. "As I looked down the hall, you could see a woman taking a right. She was in white shorts, white shirt and had a white handbag. She just turned and walked. And when we went down there and looked where she went there was only a metal wall. We couldn't find her anywhere."

Condon mentioned that he's heard an EVP of a woman in the medical area, near the tables with stirrups, saying "get out, get out." However, Condon said the agitated spirit could be saying "get it out" which could be a reference to the multiple children born on the *USS Salem*.

The executive director also told TAPS that he spotted a shadow figure in the machine shop. The ship's archivist, John Connors, said he's heard phantom footsteps above him when he's working. "It's always right above my head," Connors explained. "I go up on the main deck to see if there are any cars in the parking lot and there are no cars there, except my truck. I look around to see if anybody is onboard ... nobody."

The *Ghost Hunters* crew did pick up footsteps immediately and claimed to have heard a woman's voice. Grant Wilson said he saw a shadowy black figure creep up the gangplank. They also picked up high levels of electromagnetic activity which could result in uneasy feelings of paranoia.

During the reveal, they picked up a low-grade EVP and other inexplicable bumps in the night. "What does it come down to? We have some bangs that we can't explain and we have some low, subtle voices," said Wilson, mentioning his close encounter with the shadow figure.

"I truly believe there is something going on here," Jason Hawes confirmed. "I would like to come back and investigate."

The third USS Salem (CA-139) is one of three Des Moines-class heavy cruisers completed for the United States Navy shortly after World War II. Photo by Frank C. Grace.

If *Ghost Hunters* does return, the *USS Salem* will be secured at a different location. It's slotted to move a few docks away from its current location in Quincy. Within a one-year period, the vessel was rumored to set sail for Boston Harbor Shipyard and Marina next to the Nantucket

Lightship in East Boston and then Fall River. It was a no go for both locations. Management decided it's best to keep her close to home.

Don DeCristofaro, a paranormal investigator who spent many sleepless nights on the *USS Salem*, said he's glad the ship is staying nearby. In his opinion, the vessel is a paranormal goldmine since the *Ghost Hunters* team visited in 2009. "Interestingly, the ship became much more active after TAPS left," he said. "Numerous people claim that TAPS opened several doors for spirits on the ship and didn't close them when they left."

DeCristofaro said *Ghost Hunters* focused on the ship's least active areas, the anchor windlass room. "My most intense experiences have been in the wardroom and the mess decks. We had an evening in the wardroom where several chairs were overturned. The night was the only time I can honestly say I was uncomfortable on the ship. I really felt like something bad was with us that night."

DeCristofaro said he "lost some time" during the investigation. "The psychic I was with that night said I was channeling," he emoted. "It was very strange and I was bleeding when it was over."

Will the ghosts of the *USS Salem* continue to draw blood? As the manager of Ghost Ship Harbor's VIP paranormal experience, I tried my best not to disrespect the vessel's ghosts. No blood ... but a few of us have been scratched. Anchors aweigh.

Chapter 13

LIZZIE BORDEN'S HOUSE
FALL RIVER
MOST HAUNTED: #1

"The fact that you can sleep in the same spot where the body was found beside the bed and they keep a photo of the crime scene next to you is the cherry on top."
— Adam Berry, Destination America's *"Kindred Spirits"*

Ron Kolek, author of *Ghost Chronicles* and longtime paranormal investigator, called me after I appeared on the international version of his weekly radio show with Steven Parsons from the U.K. I asked Kolek if he had any insight as to why certain locations seemed to become progressively more active once it's featured on television. Are investigators—like the team from the Travel Channel's *Ghost Adventures*—somehow stirring up activity in a location that didn't have a history of paranormal shenanigans?

"Look at the Houghton Mansion," Kolek responded. "I investigated that place years ago before it became a regular location for paranormal groups. I've gone back there recently and it's completely different now. There's stuff there now that wasn't there before. I think these paranormal teams are bringing something with them," he said alluding to para-celeb investigators who somehow conjure negative energy at Houghton Mansion that didn't exist years ago. "Are they bringing stowaway entities with them? I think so," Kolek continued. "It's like negative spirits know where to go to get more attention."

My first thought after chatting with Kolek was the Lizzie Borden Bed & Breakfast. It's one of those locations with reported paranormal activity

The Lizzie Borden house, now a bed and breakfast, is located at 92 Second St. in Fall River. *Photo by Frank C. Grace.*

that has gotten progressively more active, and even sinister, over the years.

To be honest, I had initial reservations about listing LIzzie Borden's former home as the most haunted crime scene in Eastern Massachusetts. However, my friend Adam Berry from the new Destination America series *Kindred Spirits* quickly reconfirmed my intuition. "The fact that you can sleep in the same spot where the body was found beside the bed and they keep a photo of the crime scene next to you is the cherry on top," Berry told me online. "This crime scene still smells in my opinion."

Although she was tried and acquitted of the gruesome murder at her 1845-era Victorian home located at 92 2nd St. in Fall River, the axe-wielding Lizzie Borden never shook her "forty whacks" claim to fame that she hacked up her father and stepmother on August 4, 1892. In addition to her chop-chop notoriety, Borden apparently had an intimate relationship with actress Nance O'Neill.

There's also a theory that she had a torrid love affair with the housekeeper, Bridget Sullivan, and their testimony contradicted each other during the trial and sometimes even contradicted their own stories. Currently a bed and breakfast and museum, the Borden house is open for curiosity seekers to spend the night in the actual house where the murders took place.

As far as ghosts are concerned, visitors claim to hear sounds of a woman weeping and have spotted a full-bodied apparition wearing Victorian-era clothing dusting the furniture. There are also reports of phantom footsteps storming down the stairs and doors mysteriously opening and closing. Also, guests have heard muffled conversations coming from vacant rooms. Perhaps it's the spirits of Borden and Sullivan making a post-mortem pact to hide the bloody hatchet.

Or, maybe it's something more sinister?

In the past, I have had spirit communication dreams about Lizzie Borden's Bed & Breakfast in Fall River before I even visited the haunted crime scene.

In the dream, I saw a man with 1800s-era clothing and facial hair walk into a house with flowery wallpaper. He takes off his hat and sits on an old-school couch. The dream looked like a black-and-white 35mm and unfolded slower than the typical silent-era film. Before the man could rest his head, he looked at me and subtitles appeared, as if I was watching a film from the early 1900s. A woman appeared holding a hatchet behind her back.

The subtitle that appeared in the dream haunted me for years. It read: "Diablo did it." Then I woke up.

I didn't figure out the correlation between the house and my dream until I visited the Lizzie Borden House in 2011 while on assignment for a magazine. At the time, I was more interested in trying to solve the murder and was less focused on the message in my dream.

In hindsight, my dream seemed to be implying that the murderer—whether it was Lizzie, Bridget Sullivan or even the uncle John V. Morse—was possessed by a demonic entity.

The crew from *Ghost Adventures* investigated the house in 2011. I recently watched the episode online. The interesting part of the investigation was the paranormal research by Jeff Belanger.

"Andrew and Abby weren't even the first two Bordens to die on that property," Belanger explained. "In 1848, Andrew's uncle lived in the house right next door. His wife went nuts and drowned her three children in a well. One lived. Then she took her own life with a straight razor, slit her throat."

The investigation explored the possibility of an evil entity and the idea that the "property is plagued with dark spirits." I believe this is likely. The electronic voice phenomenon the trio allegedly captured upstairs is terrifying to me. It said: "Keep on killing. Keep 'em coming."

Another message from the spirit box said: "Tell 'em about the girl."

What girl? It's believed that Andrew Borden was communicating a message during the séance and that the message had something to do with the theory, which the psychic medium in *Ghost Adventures* discussed, that the father had an incestuous relationship with Lizzie after her mother, Sarah, died. The girl may have been one of Borden's lesbian lovers.

The uncle, John V. Morse, testified in court that the night before the murder, Lizzie had an unidentified guest in her room. He never spotted the mystery guest nor commented on the person's gender.

The murder in 1848 has fueled discussions of madness possibly running in the Borden family. In fact, the infanticide by Eliza Darling

Lizzie Borden never shook her "forty whacks" claim to fame. For the record, Borden's step-mother was struck 18 or 19 times with an axe and her father suffered 11 blows on the couch. *Photo by Frank C. Grace.*

Borden was actually brought up in Lizzie's highly publicized trial. It's believed that Eliza drowned her children in the cellar's cistern and then, possibly suffering from postpartum depression, took her own life by cutting her throat with a straight razor.

For the record, Lizzie wasn't a blood relative of Eliza and was connected to her only by marriage through her great-uncle Lawdwick.

The children, who died 44 years before Abby and Andrew were murdered, are rumored to haunt the land near the Lizzie Borden House. Guests leave dolls and other toys for ghost children who are believed to inhabit the guest rooms. There are also reports of children laughing on the second and third floors.

Another explanation of the "tell 'em about the girl" spirit-box message on *Ghost Adventures* is that it could be a reference to the murdered child, Eliza Ann Borden, who was two when she was drowned in the basement of 96 2nd St.

In other words, the girl the spirit-box message was referring to may be a ghost child.

Lee-ann Wilber, proprietor of the Lizzie Borden House, told the Bio Channel that it's common for guests to run out of the inn in fright. "I'm not used to picking up on things. They just sort of blend in now," Wilber said. "Nothing to drive me out of here."

However, in 2004 she was scared out of the house. She fell asleep on the parlor room's couch and woke at 3 a.m. and saw a shadow person. The old-school chandelier was responsible for the black mist in the hallway, she believed, but noticed a misty figure move up the staircase.

"And as I'm looking at it, it walked up the staircase," Wilber told the Bio Channel. "I said to no one in particular, 'You win tonight,' and went to sleep in my car."

Wilber said she was a skeptic when she moved in more than a decade ago. "Living here," said Wilber, "very quickly, I became a believer."

Because of its gory history, it's no surprise that the Lizzie Borden House is believed to be haunted. There have been numerous reports of cold spots in the master bedroom where Abby came face-to-face with her cold-blooded killer. There's also lore involving a former maid who quit after seeing a body-shaped indentation on the bed in Abby's room.

However, the ghostly reports have turned dark in the past few years.

My fear is that the *Ghost Adventures* lockdown may have stirred up negative energy within the house ... or possibly brought in evil from outside the building. According to several sources, the place became unusually active after the investigation.

Rachel Hoffman from Paranormal Xpeditions agreed that the crew of *Ghost Adventures* potentially conjured activity. The paranormal investigator visited the property the day after the *GAC* lockdown. "I went to Lizzie's house and opened the door and 100 black flies flew out—grown flies," Hoffman explained. "They left six hours before."

Flies, as well as shadow people, are common in a house demonstrating demonic activity. Nausea, reported by Zak Bagans and Nick Groff on *Ghost Adventures*, is also a sign of a dark force. Abby, Andrew and the maid, Bridget, and even Lizzie reported nausea hours before the two murders in 1892. Temperature fluctuations, specifically in a localized area like Abby's bedroom, have been reported in other cases of demonic infestation.

Currently a bed and breakfast and museum, Borden's house is open for curiosity seekers to spend the night in the actual location where the murders took place. *Photo by Frank C. Grace.*

Hoffman, who has investigated the Lizzie Borden House several times, said she's had experiences in the basement with her colleague Tina Storer. She also believes that Lizzie's stepmother Abby is active in the house. "I think that Abigail is there and she was indicating to us that it was an employee of her husband that murdered them," Hoffman explained. "Harper was a name we got in the basement."

In the inquest testimony of Lizzie, she mentions a nameless man who visited the house within two weeks of the double homicide. "I did not see anything. I heard the bell ring and father went to the door and let him in," Borden testified. "I did not hear anything for some time except just the voices. Then I heard the man say, 'I would like to have that place; I would like to have that store.' Father said, 'I am not willing to let your business go in there.' They talked a while and then their voices were louder and I heard father order him out and went to the front door with him."

Borden couldn't identify the out-of-town visitor. However, he should have been a person of interest.

Did Lizzie Borden do it? We'll probably never know for sure. However, it may have been dark forces conjured in the house that inspired her to do the ghastly deed. The devil once roamed here. He's waiting in the shadows of the Lizzie Borden House, patiently plotting a return.

CONCLUSION

"Sometimes you have to confront your darkest fears head on. For me, the ghosts of my past during my stint in NYC wouldn't let me go."
  — Sam Baltrusis, excerpt from the upcoming "13 Most Haunted in NYC."

I had my first experience with a negative attachment while living in New York City. During the summer of 2000, I was walking from my job on Broadway to my apartment in the East Village and I had a close encounter with something inexplicable that has haunted me for years.

It felt like the frigid hand of death grabbing my ankle.

I was casually walking through Washington Square Park, a trek I had made hundreds of times, and I clearly remember feeling something touch my ankle. I looked down thinking someone was pulling a practical joke or a homeless person was hiding in the flower bed and trying to get my attention. No one was there.

I kept walking and then I felt it again. The second time was more profound as the disembodied hand frantically held on and I remembered reaching down to physically knock off the death grip of someone who was definitely not there.

I didn't tell a soul. I thought it was something explainable. Then it happened again.

It was a particularly warm winter day a few months later and right around the same spot, the corner of Washington Square Park East, is where I felt the mysterious hand again. This time it wasn't letting go.

I didn't even think about the possibility of it being a ghost. At this point in my life I was wearing what I call "paranormal blinders" and quickly tried to shrug off the incident.

In 1889, to celebrate the centennial of George Washington's inauguration as president of the United States, a large plaster and wood Memorial Arch was erected over Fifth Avenue just north of the Washington Square Park. *Photo by Jason Baker.*

In hindsight, I believe the spirit was desperately trying to tell me something. Or worse, it was trying to attach himself to me.

Joni Mayhan, author of *Dark and Scary Things*, told me that it's possible that the ghost I encountered at Washington Square Park was preying on my sensitivity to the paranormal.

"I've had a few really horrible attachments," explained Mayhan. "One of them was the subject of my book *Soul Collector*."

Mayhan said sensitives are like beacons of light to the spirit realm. "Since everybody senses them differently, it's always difficult to say if you had an attachment or not. One big sign though is a personality change or sudden depression. Dark moods and a feeling of just not wanting to live anymore are pretty common. They don't have to touch us to attach to us, but it probably doesn't hurt. They've penetrated our shield."

After the second encounter in Washington Square Park, my mood did change. In fact, I was overwhelmed by negativity. I mysteriously started having issues with anxiety and would drink alcohol to self-medicate. It was as if the icy hand of death had pulled me into the abyss. I was drowning with negative emotions and my life started to spiral out of control.

It felt like the attachment was feeding off of my energy.

"Investigators often flock to haunted venues, needlessly paying tremendous amounts of money to hunt for a ghost, while passing several dozen ghosts on their way to the door. Ghosts are everywhere," Mayhan continued. "You'll find them lurking in places where you find groups of people. Shopping malls and movie theaters are prime locations, as are restaurants, hospitals and churches. Most of the time the ghosts are happy to remain there, but occasionally they find one human they feel is worth following."

I've mentioned my first-hand encounter in NYC at various book signings including a recent speaking engagement at the Massachusetts State House. One of the guests at the event mentioned to me that the skeletal remains of hundreds of bodies were uncovered in Washington Square Park. I couldn't breathe.

I packed my bags and returned to a city that I called home for more than eight years. NYC almost destroyed me. After a series of traumatic events including a violent mugging on a subway platform and then the horrific devastation of 9/11, I became a shell of person in the months after my face-to-face encounter in Washington Square Park. After intensive therapy and then six years of sobriety in Boston, I was in a better mental place. I had to see for myself if the unmarked graves buried beneath the park were related to the disembodied hand I felt on my ankle in 2000.

Sometimes you have to confront your darkest fears head on. For me, the ghosts of my past during my stint in NYC wouldn't let me go.

I needed closure. It was time.

The is the introduction to author Sam Baltrusis's upcoming *13 Most Haunted in New York City*. Photo by Jason Baker.

My first experience with Manhattan was in 1988. My high school band from the Florida Panhandle performed at the Macy's Thanksgiving Day Parade. The city was electric. In fact, my crew of fellow musicians visited a few haunts from my upcoming *13 Most Haunted in New York City* including Ellis Island. I remember walking with my friends in the heart of Times Square at night and intuitively knowing I would someday live in the city that never sleeps.

I was smitten with the Big Apple. It was love at first bite.

I moved to Boston in the 1990's for college. A friend from my freshman year at Boston University transferred to New York University.

She invited me to visit and encouraged me to check out the Washington Square Park parade of freaks during Halloween. It was edgier back then and I remember larger-than-life puppets and furry, four-legged creatures parading through what I now call NYC's "haunted corridor."

My friend introduced me to the Village's haunted history. Around the corner from her dorm was where my childhood hero, Edgar Allan Poe, penned the final draft to his classic *The Raven* as well as my favorite tale from that era, *The Cask of the Amontillado*. Nowadays, NYU's Furman Hall has taken over the historic 85 West Third St. location. The three-story building where Poe lived for eight months from 1844 to 1845 was torn down in 2001.

All that remains is the façade of his former home and what some say is the Boston-bred icon's ghost. There's a lamppost in front of the allegedly haunted structure and according to the website *Curbed*, "Poe's ghost has been seen climbing it by spooked law students."

Has his ghost been spotted recently? According to multiple sources the answer is, well, "nevermore."

Literally across West Third Street is another well-documented haunt, Fire Patrol Station No. 2. According to ghost lore, there are reports of a firehouse phantom with 1930s-era clothing, graying hair and a mustache. He's also been spotted wearing firefighting gear and people inside have seen him put on an old-school helmet as if he's suiting up for an alarm. The ghost, identified by a supposed psychic as Firefighter Schwartz. "He supposedly hanged himself on the fourth floor after he discovered that his wife was being unfaithful," wrote Tom Ogden in *Haunted Greenwich Village*. "This occurred sometime in the decade before World War II—which would explain why his attire dated from that period."

The tall tale snowballed with multiple sightings in the 1990s. One firefighter claimed to have had a face-to-face encounter with the phantom fireman in 1992 saying the ghost leaned over him while he napped on the second floor. Visitors to the structure reported feeling tapped by an unseen force on the spiral staircase and objects would mysteriously move, like a 150-pound dolly, without explanation.

CNN anchor, Anderson Cooper, purchased the old firehouse located at 84 West Third Street in 2009. According to a source who chatted with Cooper, the Firefighter Schwartz ghost story was completely fabricated.

And, no, he hasn't had a close encounter with the ghostly mustachioed gent. At least, not yet.

I spent the summer of 1993 at the NYU dorm on Third Avenue while interning at *Seventeen* magazine. I remember spending many afternoons in Washington Square Park, reading and jotting down observations in my notebook. One line I wrote still haunts me: "This is where the dead people go." In hindsight, I'm not sure what I was referring to, but I did feel a magnetic force summon me back day after day.

I found out years later that the area was a dead man's dumping ground. In fact, over 20,000 people were buried in the park and some estimate that the numbers could be as high as 125,000.

"Washington Square Park became a public park in 1827," reported the online source *Curbed*. "The park, located in the Village and surrounded by NYU, was once home to a graveyard. In 1797, the land was acquired by the Common Council for use as a potter's field and a place for public executions. Some historians think that the land might also have been used as a cemetery for one of the adjacent churches, as headstones have been unearthed in the park."

When I returned to my old stomping grounds in November 2015, the rumored skeletal remains from a hidden burial vault at the corner of Washington Square Park East and Waverly Place were uncovered while crews were updating the city's century-old water main system. "We're hoping now to confirm what the descendent church might be," said Alyssa Loorya, president of Chrysalis Archaeological Consultants, adding that the vaults date back to the late 1700s up to the early 18th century. "You normally don't find burial vaults beneath the city streets."

Based on the city's policy, crews had to leave the skeletal remains as they found them. Returning to the scene, you could see what looked like bones from the exposed vaults covered with makeshift pieces of plywood. While walking past these death pits with photographer Jason Baker, I had the sensation of an energy passing through my body for just a second and then quickly leave.

It was a familiar tingling sensation. "Something just passed through me," I said out loud. There was a jolt of electricity and then I felt drained. I'm shivering in the beauty and the madness of the moment.

City workers uncovered a 19th century burial vault – which then led to the finding of a second tomb – containing skeletal remains beneath the edge of Washington Square Park. *Photo by Frank C. Grace.*

"Ghosts will pull energy where they can find it," explained author Joni Mayhan. "A typical sign that a ghost is using your energy is the sensation of vibration. When they pull energy from us, sometimes their vibrational rate is different from ours, giving us the feeling that we are vibrating from the inside out."

I looked up at the Washington Square arch. To the right was a larger-than-life moon, only a few days after the last full one before the winter solstice. Native Americans called it the "moon when deer shed antlers." It's also known as the "mourning moon."

At this point, I unexpectedly did something that has taken me years to completely understand. I decided to let go. The only true negative attachment I had was the self-constructed prison I created in my head.

"It's time to face your shadow self," whispered a voice in the darkness. The ghosts of my past will no longer haunt me.

SOURCES

I updated excerpts from my first four books including *Ghosts of Boston: Haunts of the Hub* and *Ghosts of Salem: Haunts of the Witch City* and *13 Most Haunted in Massachusetts* were featured in *13 Most Haunted Crime Scenes Beyond Boston*. The material in this book is drawn from published sources, including issues of *Boston Spirit*, *Stuff* magazine, *Boston Globe*, *Boston Herald*, *Metrowest Daily*, *The New York Times*, *Patriot Ledger*, *SouthCoast Today*, *MATV's Neighborhood View* and television programs like the Travel Channel's *Ghost Adventures* and Syfy's *Ghost Hunters*. Several books on the Bay State's paranormal history were used and cited throughout the text. Other New England–based websites and periodicals, like my various newspaper and magazine articles on the paranormal, Joni Mayhan's work for Ghost Diaries and Peter Muise's blog *New England Folklore* served as primary sources. I also conducted firsthand interviews, and some of the material is drawn from my own research. The Boston-based ghost tour, Boston Haunts, was also a major source and generated original content. My tours in Salem, Cambridge, Boston Harbor and Provincetown also served as inspiration for the book. It should be noted that ghost stories are subjective, and I have made a concerted effort to stick to the historical facts, even if it resulted in debunking an alleged encounter with the paranormal.

Baltrusis, Sam. *Ghosts of Boston: Haunts of the Hub*. Charleston, SC: The History Press, 2012.
Baltrusis, Sam. *Ghosts of Cambridge: Haunts of Harvard Square and Beyond*. Charleston, SC: The History Press, 2013.
Baltrusis, Sam. *Ghosts of Salem: Haunts of the Witch City*. Charleston, SC: The History Press, 2014.
Balzano, Christopher. *Dark Woods: Cults, Crime, and the Paranormal in the Freetown State Forest*, Massachusetts. Atglen, PA: Schiffer Publishing, 2007.

D'Agostino, Thomas. *A Guide to Haunted New England*. Charleston, SC: The History Press, 2009.

Forest, Christopher. *North Shore Spirits of Massachusetts*. Atglen, PA: Schiffer Publishing, 2003.

Gellerman, Bruce and Sherman, Erik. *Massachusetts Curiosities*. Guilford, CT: The Globe Pequot Press, 2005.

Hall, Thomas. *Shipwrecks of Massachusetts Bay*. Charleston, SC: The History Press, 2012.

Hauk, Dennis William. *Haunted Places: The National Directory*. New York: Penguin Group, 1996.

Jasper, Mark. *Haunted Cape Cod & The Islands*. Yarmouthport, MA: On Cape Publications, 2002.

Jasper, Mark. *Haunted Inns of New England*. Yarmouthport, MA: On Cape Publications, 2000.

Mayhan, Joni. *Dark and Scary Things*. Gardner, MA: Joni Mayhan, 2015.

Muise, Peter. *Legends and Lore of the North Shore*. Charleston, SC: The History Press, 2014.

Nadler, Holly Mascott. *Ghosts of Boston Town: Three Centuries of True Hauntings*. Camden, ME: Down East Books, 2002.

Norman, Michael and Scott, Beth. *Historic Haunted America*. New York, NY: Tor Books, 1995.

Ogden, Tom. *The Complete Idiot's Guide to Ghosts & Hauntings*. Indianapolis, IN: Alpha Books, 2004.

Revai, Cheri. *Haunted Massachusetts: Ghosts and Strange Phenomena of the Bay State*. Mechanicsburg, PA: Stackpole Books, 2005.

ABOUT THE AUTHOR

Sam Baltrusis, author of *Ghosts of Boston, Ghosts of Salem* and *13 Most Haunted in Massachusetts*, is the former editor in chief of several regional publications, including *Spare Change News, Scout Somerville* and *Scout Cambridge*. He has been featured as Boston's paranormal expert on the Biography Channel's *Haunted Encounters*. As a side gig, Baltrusis moonlights as a guide. He has launched the successful ghost tours Boston Haunts and Cambridge Haunts and spearheaded the Salem Cursed? Walking Tour. Baltrusis is also a sought-after lecturer who speaks at dozens of paranormal-related events scattered throughout New England, including an author discussion at the Massachusetts State House. In the past, he has worked for VH1, MTV.com, *Newsweek*, ABC Radio and as a regional stringer for the *New York Times*. 13MostHaunted.com for more information.

After a road trip to some of the state's most haunted locations, author Sam Baltrusis enjoys a breathtaking view from the Wigwam Western Summit in North Adams. *Photo by Frank C. Grace.*

13 Most Haunted

Made in the USA
Lexington, KY
10 March 2017